St. Lucia's Julius Caesar & Marcus Brutus

A St. Lucian Political Epic

JOHN COMPTON
& GEORGE ODLUM

By Martinus François

Order this book online at www.trafford.com
or email orders@trafford.com

Most Trafford titles are also available at major online book retailers.

Note for Librarians: A cataloguing record for this book is available from Library
and Archives Canada at www.collectionscanada.ca/amicus/index-e.html

Printed in Victoria, BC, Canada.

ISBN: 978-1-4251-8996-9 (sc)

*Our mission is to efficiently provide the world's finest, most comprehensive book publishing
service, enabling every author to experience success. To find out how to publish your
book, your way, and have it available worldwide, visit us online at www.trafford.com*

Trafford rev. 09/15/2010

 www.trafford.com

North America & international
toll-free: 1 888 232 4444 (USA & Canada)
phone: 250 383 6864 ♦ fax: 812 355 4082

Acknowledgement

The author acknowledges the authors, publishers and writers of the various passages and articles used in this book as well as the families of the late Sir John George Melvin Compton and George William Odlum respectively for the photos.

Dedication

This book is dedicated to the memory of Sir John George Melvin Compton, who passed away on September 7, 2006 and George William Odlum, who passed away on September 28, 2003 in commemoration of St. Lucia's 30th anniversary of political independence on February 22, 2009

All the world's a stage
And all the men and women merely players:
They have their exits and their entrances:
And one man in his time
plays many parts....

Contents

Prologue		vii
Part I:	The Roman Julius Caesar	1
Part II:	Shakespeare's *Julius Caesar*	9
Part III:	St. Lucia's Julius Caesar	23
Part IV:	St. Lucia's Marcus Brutus	37
Epilogue I:	St. Lucia's Marcus Brutus	67
Epilogue II:	St. Lucia's Julius Caesar	101

Prologue

St. Lucia's Julius Caesar & Marcus Brutus is based on Shakespeare's play, *Julius Caesar*, which is based on true historical accounts of the origins, execution and consequences of the assassination of the Roman dictator, Julius Caesar.

Shakespeare's purpose in writing the play in 1599 A.D. was not simply to serve as an exact historical reconstruction of the murder of Julius Caesar in 44 B.C. The historical material was only as relevant as what the artist made of it. That he made a play of universal human interest is supported by the fact that it has lost none of its germs of reality, even in the XXI century; and is capable of engaging the attention of diverse audiences – whether or not they are compelled by the exigencies of university examinations in English literature.

Julius Caesar is an important work of art which focuses on a particular vision of life and contributes not solely to an evening's theatrical entertainment but also to a bold and imaginative statement about something of lasting importance and universality. On the one hand, Shakespeare presents Roman political society flourishing under a Monarchy in all but name ruled by Julius Caesar with an iron fist. Against this background, he sets a group of men under the leadership of Marcus Brutus who <u>are</u> convinced that such political organization is dangerous to Roman public interest and from which Rome must be liberated in order to preserve its status as a Republic – a country which is governed without Kings, Queens or Emperors.

Shakespeare brings these two concepts to the test and makes it clear that the criterion to be kept in mind in judging the efficacy and justice of any system of Government is the welfare of the society concerned. With these principles established, the resolution of the problem begins.

The play explores themes which were as relevant in the playwright's time as they are today. For example, the two great revolutionary movements towards the end of the 18th century, the American Revolution in 1776 and the French Revolution in 1789, had their intellectual causes in Republican ideals such as; the belief that the State is a necessary evil, that Government must rest on the consent of the governed, that the doctrine of popular sovereignty must be paramount, as well as the importance of the fundamental rights and freedoms of citizens.

Shakespeare's *Julius Caesar* might well have provided the inspiration upon which these revolutionary movements professed to rest. Both the American founding fathers and the French were convinced that their actions were susceptible of justification in terms of the venerable ideals of republicanism – in other words, the past as prologue to the future.

St. Lucia's Julius Caesar & Marcus Brutus not only brilliantly caricatures John Compton and George Odlum – St. Lucia's twin political legends of the pre-independence and post-independence periods – as Shakespeare's Julius Caesar and Marcus Brutus respectively as a bold and imaginative statement in itself; but the book also makes a bold and imaginative statement as to where we are at politically, where we wish to go; and the process or processes that are required to take us there.

This book is timely and important for three reasons: firstly, it helps us to properly assess the importance and scale of the changes that are required in our Government and politics as it becomes increasingly imperative for our future that we stand and take stock of what appears to be a country looking for an appropriate political system as well as sound principles and values to guide its quest for development in the XXI century;

secondly, it helps us to relate the need for a new concept of how Government is organized to the wider crisis in our politics; and thirdly, it assists us in envisioning the political algebra and the cultural, social and economic equations that link our past and present to the future.

PART I
THE ROMAN JULIUS CAESAR

Like Hercules, citizens, they said just now
He had sought the laurel at the cost of death;
Returning from Spain, seeking his household gods, Caesar
has conquered
After sacrifice to the just gods, let his
Wife come forth, happy for her matchless husband,
And the sister of our famous leader, and,
Wearing the bands of
Suppliants, mothers of young men and maidens
Who are now safe....

Horace, *Odes,* III.xiv

Julius Caesar, the ancient Roman dictator, was born in 100 B.C., to become the most famous of all the Romans: soldier, statesman, orator and historian. Rome was a Republic, a country governed without a King or Queen or Emperor.

Rome was founded about 1000 B.C. by Italic peoples who lived in the district of Latium, south of the Tiber River. During this early period of Roman civilization, the Romans appear to have been more interested in authority and stability rather than liberty or democracy.

Rome was essentially an extension of the idea of the patriarchal family; with the King exercising jurisdiction over his subjects similar to that of the head of the family over the members of his household. But just as the authority of the father was limited by law and custom and by the requirement that he must respect the wishes of his adult sons, the sovereignty of the King was limited by the ancient constitution which he was powerless to change without the consent of the chieftains of the realm. His prerogatives were more executive and judicial than legislative. He punished men for breaches of order; usually with the penalty of death or flogging. He judged all civil and criminal cases but he had no authority to pardon without the consent of the parliamentary Assembly. Although his accession to office had to be confirmed by the people, he could not be deposed. Neither was there anyone who could challenge the exercise of his regal powers.

Roman Government of this time consisted not only of the Monarchy but there were also an Assembly and a Senate. As one of the chief sources of sovereign power, the Assembly was made up of all the male citizens of military age. This body had an absolute veto on any proposal for a change in the law which the King might make. It also had the power to determine whether pardons should be granted and whether aggressive war should be declared. But still it was nevertheless a ratifying body with no right to initiate legislation or recommend changes of policy. Nor could its members speak unless they were invited to do so by the King.

The Senate was a kind of council of elders; comprising in its membership the heads of the various clans of the realm. The Senators embodied the sovereign power of the State more than the common citizens. The King was but one of their number to whom they had delegated the active exercise of their authority. When the royal office became vacant, the powers of the King immediately reverted to the Senate until the succession of the new Monarch had been confirmed by the people.

The Senate was a very conservative body whose chief function was to examine proposals of the King which had been ratified by the Assembly and to veto them if they violated rights established by ancient custom; thereby making it almost impossible for fundamental changes to be made in the law even when the majority of citizens were ready to sanction them.

The Monarchy was overthrown towards the end of the 6th century B.C. because of senatorial jealousy and an oligarchic Republic set up as the aristocracy moved to gain a monopoly of power for itself.

The revolution which overthrew the Monarchy was just about as conservative as it is possible for a revolution to be. Its chief effect was to substitute two elected consuls for the King and to exalt the position of the Senate by vesting it with control over the public funds and with a veto over all actions of the Assembly. The consuls were themselves members of the senatorial class. They did not rule jointly, but each was supposed to possess the full executive and judicial authority which had hitherto been wielded by the King. If a conflict arose between them, the Senate would be called upon to adjudicate; or, in time of crisis or emergency, a dictator would be appointed for an interim period of 6 months In all other respects, the Government remained the same as in the days of the Monarchy.

It was not long after the establishment of the Republic that a power struggle ensued between the patricians and the plebeians – the two great classes of the Roman population. The patricians were wealthy landowners and members of the aristocratic class. They monopolized the Senate seats and the offices of the magistracy.

On the other hand, the plebeians were the common citizens of Rome – small farmers, craftsmen and tradesmen. Many were clients and dependents of the patricians; obliged to fight for them, to render them political support and to cultivate their estates in return for protection.

The grievances of the plebeians that sparked off the revolt were manifold; they were excluded from all aspects of the Government of Rome, except membership in the Assembly, even though they were compelled to pay heavy taxes and forced to serve in the army in time of war; they did not know their legal rights and were discriminated against in judicial trials; the laws were unwritten, and no one but the consuls had the power to interpret them; in suits for debt the patrician creditor was frequently allowed to sell the plebeian debtor into slavery.

It was in order to obtain a redress of these grievances that the plebeians rebelled soon after the beginning of the 5th century B.C. The first victory of the plebeians was realized in 470 B.C., when they forced the patricians to agree to the election of a number of tribunes with power to protect the citizens by means of a veto over unlawful acts of the magistrates. This victory was followed in 450 B.C. by a successful demand for codification of the laws; thus enabling the people to know where they stood in relation to the law. It also permitted an appeal to the Assembly against a magistrate's sentence of capital punishment.

About a generation later the plebeians won eligibility to positions as lay magistrates; and in 362 B.C., the first plebeian consul was elected; thereby breaking the patrician monopoly of seats in the Senate; what with the fact that ancient Roman custom provided that consuls, upon completing their term of office, should automatically enter the Senate.

The ultimate victory of the plebeians came in 287 B.C. with the passage of the Hortensian Law (named after the dictator Quintus Hortensius), which provided that measures enacted by the Assembly should become binding upon the State whether the Senate approved them or not.

The period from 146 B.C. to the accession of Julius Caesar in 46 B.C. was one of the most turbulent in the history of Rome. Bitter class conflicts, assassinations, desperate power struggles between rival dictators, wars, civil wars and insurrections were common occurrences of this period

The first stage in the conflict between classes of citizens came with the revolt of the Gracchi who were mainly spokesmen for the landless farmers against the senatorial aristocracy; although they were able to recruit some middle-class support. In 133 B.C., Tiberius Gracchus, having been elected tribune, persuaded the Assembly to enact a law limiting the amount of land which any person might hold to about 300 acres and providing that the excess should be surrendered to the State for lease to poor citizens at a nominal rental.

But Gracchus' term expired before the law could be put into effect; whereupon he determined to stand for re-election in defiance of the constitutional provision limiting his term to 1 year. But this played straight into the hands of the Senators; they used Gracchus' illegal move as an excuse to resort to violence. The elections were accompanied by riots in which Tiberius and 300 of his followers were slaughtered by clients and slaves of the aristocracy.

A decade later, Gaius Gracchus, the younger brother of Tiberius, renewed the struggle for the underprivileged. Having been elected in 123 B.C., he procured the enactment of a law which provided for a monthly distribution of grain to the people of the city at one-half the market price.

Next he prepared an attack upon the powers of the Senate but he was defeated in his bid for re-election and branded an enemy of the State by the Senate. When he refused to stand trial before the Senate, a state of war was proclaimed against him. After his followers had been defeated, Gaius persuaded a faithful slave to kill him. Subsequently, 3,000 of his adherents were condemned to death.

About 60 B.C., several new military leaders emerged to espouse the cause of the people; the most famous of them were Pompey and Julius Caesar. For a time they pooled their energies and resources in a plot to gain control of the Government; but later, they became rivals and sought to outdo each other in bids for popular support.

Pompey won fame when he conquered Syria and Palestine; while Caesar devoted his talents to a series of brilliant forays against the Gauls in Western Europe; annexing to the Roman State the territory of modern Belgium and France.

In 52 B.C., after a series of mob disorders in Rome, Pompey was elected sole consul, with the backing of the Senate; and Caesar branded an enemy of the State. Pompey had conspired with the senatorial faction to deprive Caesar of political power. The result was a deadly war between the two men.

In 49 B.C., with the famous pronouncement "The die is cast", Caesar crossed the Rubicon (a small river in eastern Italy that was part of the boundary between the Roman Republic and its provinces) and started the civil war that made him master of Rome. (Today, the phrase "Cross the Rubicon" is used to denote a course of action from which one cannot turn back.)

Therefore, Julius Caesar crossed the Rubicon and began a march on Rome. Pompey fled to the East in an attempt to mobilize a large enough army to regain control of Italy. In 48 B.C., rival forces of the two men clashed at Pharsalus in Thessaly. Pompey was defeated and later murdered by agents of the King of Egypt.

After his victory, Julius Caesar returned to Rome; there was now no one who dared to challenge his power. He cowed the Senate into granting his every whim and fancy. In 46 B.C., he became dictator for 10 years; and, in the following year, for life. In addition, he assumed nearly every other magisterial title that would augment his power; he was consul, tribune, censor, and supreme pontiff.

He got from the Senate full authority to make war and peace and to control the revenues of the State. For all practical purposes, Julius Caesar was above the law; and the other agents of the Government merely his servants.

Over the centuries, students of Roman history have generally believed that Caesar fully intended to re-establish the Monarchy and make himself King. In fact, it was on such a charge that he was assassinated in 44 B.C. by a group of conspirators under the leadership of Marcus Brutus; representing the old senatorial aristocracy that had overthrown the King in the 6th century B.C.

PART II
SHAKESPEARE'S *JULIUS CAESAR*

Shakespeare's plays can be classified as comedies, tragedies or histories; a comedy is a play with a happy ending; a tragedy, which might be the result of weakness of character or a series of events which are beyond control, ends less happily than a comedy; histories are based on historical characters and events, and because they are re-enactments of real life, some histories can be said to be either comedies or tragedies. In 1959, Shakespeare wrote the play, *Julius Caesar*, based on true historical accounts of the origins, execution and consequences of the assassination of Julius Caesar.

The play opens with the benevolent dictator celebrating his latest military triumph. There are still Pompey sympathizers in high places; most notably Marcus Brutus to whom Caesar has been magnanimous in victory; in fact, the dictator has promoted Brutus. These members of the senatorial class are convinced that Caesar is about to re-establish the Monarchy, which was overthrown in the 6th century B.C., and declare himself King of Rome.

At the feast to honour the dictator's latest military victory, not all the guests are happy at the way things are moving. The Republican senatorial partisans are secretly opposed to Caesar's growing power. Their fears are not helped by the fact that, during the celebrations, Mark Anthony, a Caesar loyalist, has offered the dictator a mock crown, which the dictator refuses. The Republicans are, nevertheless, not fooled and interpret this as planting the idea, in the minds of the people, of Julius Caesar becoming King.

The instigator and dynamic force behind the conspiracy is Cassius; who envies Caesar his greatness. He plays upon the fears of Brutus, a noble and respectable Roman, about the monarchical intentions of Caesar:

> CAESAR: *Let me have men about me that are fat;*
> *Sleek-headed men and such as sleep o'nights;*
> *Young Cassius has a lean and hungry look;*
> *He thinks too much; such men are dangerous.*

Shakespeare's *Julius Caesar:* Act I, Scene II

After all, Cassius reckons, what in the name of Caesar that makes him so great and informs Brutus that "in these days of oppressive Government", many look to him, the noble Brutus, for leadership.

Brutus remarks that as far as he is concerned he would prefer relative obscurity than to serve under an oppressive tyranny and would give some thought to his proposal:

> BRUTUS: *Brutus had rather be a villager,*
> *Than to repute himself a son of Rome;*
> *Under these hard conditions as this time:*
> *Is like to lay upon us.*

Shakespeare's *Julius Caesar:* Act I, Scene II

In a closing monologue, Cassius brags that he has managed to seduce the naïve Brutus from loyalty to his benefactor. He departs, taking upon himself what so often falls to the lot of the devoted organizer – the production and distribution of literature.

Cassius' own motive appears to be ambivalent: on the one hand, he claims to have strong republican convictions and is opposed to the rule of a King or tyrant; on the other hand, he also appears to have a personal grudge against Caesar whom he unkindly regards as a man inferior to himself and who possesses no natural right to be master of Rome. It is this combination of motives that gives him his fierce energy in driving him towards the assassination:

> CASSIUS: *Upon what meat doth this our Caesar feed,*
> *That he is grown so great?*
> *The fault, dear Brutus, is not in our stars,*
> *But in ourselves, that we are underlings.*

Shakespeare's *Julius Caesar*: Act I, Scene III

But whether Cassius is genuinely motivated by political principles, or simply personal malice; he knows that the truly idealistic Brutus would be moved by even a profession of political idealism, no matter how false. And he desperately needs to enlist Brutus' support for the success of his enterprise.

Cassius persuades Brutus that by killing Caesar is the only way to save the Republic from Caesar's monarchical ambitions. Reluctantly, Brutus buys into the plot and, because of his charisma, becomes leader.

Whereas Cassius is ambivalent in his motives, Brutus is, throughout the period before the assassination, in a state of agonized indecision: on the one hand, he prides himself as a man of high political principles and ideals who will not tolerate the notion of a despotic King; on the other hand, he is a scrupulous man to whom the thought of committing murder is naturally repugnant; especially the murder of a man who is not only his benefactor but a close friend.

There ensued a raging agony between Brutus' heart and his mind; between his love of Caesar and his love for Rome. It's as if he is hearing a little voice inside of him saying "You have a respectable position in Caesar's kingdom and doing quite well for yourself; and Julius Caesar is not so bad, after all – never mind Cassius". While another little voice is saying "Are you going to stand idly by and apathetically watch Caesar become Rome's greatest nightmare?"

He must divorce personal friendship from public interest; a parallel separation between the man and the statesman. After all, it is not uncommon that in matters of policy or public interest people are forced to take an opposing stand against men whom they otherwise like and respect. This can be seen in the management of any organization; including politics.

In the final analysis, Brutus is forced to make a choice between two equally unacceptable alternatives: he can either refrain from allying himself with Cassius and thereby betray his high political ideals; or join the conspiracy and thereby betray his friendship with Caesar:

> BRUTUS: *It must be by his death: and for my part,*
> *I know no personal cause to spurn at him,*
> *But for the general. He would be crown'd:*
> *How that might change his nature, there's the*
> *question.*

Shakespeare's *Julius Caesar*: Act II, Scene I

So Brutus decrees death to Caesar's ambition to be crowned King of Rome; rationalizing that Caesar has reached dangerously close to the limits of the power delegated to him under the Republican constitution. Although the dictator presently lives within the four corners of the constitution; but motivated by higher ambition, he now threatens to reject, in theory as well as in practice, the very system through which he rose to his position of power:

> BRUTUS: *But 'tis common proof*
> *That lowliness is young ambition's ladder,*
> *Whereto the climber-upward turns his face;*
> *But when he once attains the upmost rung,*
> *He then unto the ladder turns his back,*
> *Looks in the clouds, scorning the base degrees*
> *By which he did ascend.*

Shakespeare's *Julius Caesar*: Act II, Scene I

Shakespeare might have been influenced by George Buchanan, his contemporary 16th century advocate of limited Monarchy, who believed that "rulers should be constrained to make use not of their own licentious wills in judgement, but of that right or privilege which the people had conferred upon them".

Julius Caesar, now a benefit to Rome, can easily become a menace if the crown establishes the sovereignty of his own "licentious will" to run amuck. As he reasons it out:

> BRUTUS: *So Caesar may;*
> *Then, lest he may, prevent.*

Shakespeare's *Julius Caesar*: Act II, Scene I

The use of such murderous violence to preserve the sovereignty of the old Republican system is justified, Brutus reckons, because the public interest and the welfare of Rome demands it. The major premise with which his monologue opens confirms the principled honesty of his intentions: "*I have no personal cause to spurn at him/But for the general.*"

It is only by preventing the coronation of a despotic King can the general, or common, good be preserved. To him, the rule of one man reduces the rest of us to slaves.

After Caesar is killed, none of the conspirators appears to have given any thought to the consequences of their actions. The conspirators are in a quandary as to their next course of action – whether to prepare to defend themselves or boldly proclaim their crusade from the rostrum outside. Brutus rescues them from this state of indecision with an unwise sacramental gesture that they smear their arms and weapons with the dead dictator's blood in order to raise them aloft in the eye of the public as a red sign of their emancipation from slavery; foolishly assuming that by destroying a tyrant, they have at once initiated a new era of peace, freedom and liberty:

CINNA: *Liberty! Freedom! Tyranny is dead!*
        Run hence, proclaim, cry it about the streets.

BRUTUS: *Let's all cry "Peace, Freedom, and Liberty!"*

CASSIUS: *Some to the common pulpits, and cry out:*
          Liberty! Freedom! and Enfranchisement!
          So oft as that shall be,
          So oft shall the knot of us be call'd
          The men that gave their country LIBERTY!

Shakespeare's *Julius Caesar*: Act III, Scene I

The killing of Caesar having been accomplished, the fruits of it are spoiled by the overgenerous character of Brutus who, not only unwisely spares the life of Mark Anthony, a close associate of Caesar; but rather unadvisedly allows him to deliver a eulogy at his master's funeral – against the wishes of the sharper and more cynical Cassius who instinctively foresees the dangerous purposes to which Anthony may use his funeral oration over Caesar's dead body. This results in a brief struggle

of wills between Brutus' and Cassius'; Brutus' will prevails –
with disastrous consequences.

The stage is now set for the delivery of two funeral eulogies
on which may turn the success or failure of the palace coup. The
coup plotters will try to justify their radical action in the face
of public opinion while Mark Anthony will try to turn public
opinion against the plotters.

Brutus delivers his eulogy and is warmly received:

BRUTUS: *Romans, countrymen, and lovers!*
            Hear me for my cause, and be silent, that you
            may hear.
            Believe me for mine honour, and have respect to
            mine honour, that you may believe.
            Censure me in your wisdom, and awake your
            senses, that you may the better judge.
            If there be any in this assembly, any dear friend of
            Caesar's, to him I say that Brutus' love to Caesar
            was no less than his.
            If then that friend demand why Brutus rose
            against Caesar, this is my answer;
            Not that I lov'd Caesar less, but that I lov'd Rome
            more.
            Had you rather Caesar were living, and die all
            slaves, than that Caesar were dead, to live all free
            men?
            As Caesar lov'd me, I weep for him; as he was
            fortunate, I rejoiced at it, as he was valiant, I
            honour him; as he was ambitious, I slew him.
            There is tears for his love; joy for his fortune:
            honour for his valour; and death for his
            ambition.

Shakespeare's *Julius Caesar*: Act III, Scene II

Brutus' appeal to the crowd is in prose. His language is of logic and of reason – his love of Caesar is equal to that of anyone in the assembly but his love for Rome is greater. He tells his audience that they would have been slaves – slavery under Caesar or freedom after his death.

Brutus makes a tactical mistake in assuming that the crowd is as rational as he. He relies on his own credit and reputation and asks the crowd to trust his judgment.

Anthony appeals directly to his audience's feelings:

ANTHONY: *This was the most unkindest cut of all,*
　　　For when the noble Caesar saw him stab,
　　　Ingratitude, more strong than traitor's arms,
　　　Quite vanquished him: then burst his mighty heart;
　　　And, in his mantle muffling up his face,
　　　Even at the base of Pompey's statua,
　　　Which all the while ran blood, great Caesar fell.
　　　O! what a fall was there, my countrymen.

Shakespeare's *Julius Caesar*: Act III, Scene II

Anthony uses powerful oratory to convince the crowd that Caesar has been wronged by the conspirators and must be avenged. His appeal is emotional and in verse – Caesar has been slain for bringing fame and glory to Rome.

Anthony's rabble-rousing demagoguery has whipped up the emotions of the now angry mob to a heightened state of hysteria as they demand mob justice against Brutus and his co-conspirators. By the time Anthony finishes his speech, Brutus and Cassius have fled into the provinces as mutiny and civil war engulf Rome.

Instead of benefiting his country, Brutus has plunged it into civil war; albeit acting from the best motives and the highest of principles. In a play full of scenes of persuasion and crises of choice, the Roman citizens are confronted with a choice between believing Brutus' portrayal of Caesar as a borderline tyrant and Anthony's depiction of him as a benevolent man. They choose to believe the latter account – not because it is necessarily the truth but because it is more emotively conveyed.

The subsequent events suggest a rapid decline in justification for the conspirators' cause as their fall is seen as inevitable.

The final section of the play is dominated by a clash of temperaments between Brutus' and Cassius'; an incompatibility that was apparent from the beginning but which Shakespeare now highlights in the famous "Quarrel Scene".

Now both fugitives, Cassius accuses Brutus of ignoring a letter from him in support of one of Cassius' men who is said to have taken bribes. Brutus accuses Cassius of taking bribes himself and reminds him that Caesar was killed in the name of justice. Cassius becomes angry and threatens Brutus but the latter is unmoved. He further reminds Cassius that he has asked for gold to pay his army and this request Cassius has refused:

BRUTUS: *The name of Cassius honours this corruption*
           And chastisement doth therefore hide his head.

CASSIUS: *Chastisement!*

BRUTUS: *Did not great Julius bleed for justice's sake?*
           What villain touch'd his body, that did stab,
           And not for justice? What, shall one of us,
           That strucke the foremost man of all this world
           But for supporting Robbers, shall we now
           Contaminate our fingers with base bribes?

CASSIUS: *Do not presume too much upon my love;*
           I may do that I shall be sorry for.

> BRUTUS: *You have done that you should be sorry for.*
> *There is no terror, Cassius, in your threats;*
> *For I am arm'd so strong in honesty*
> *That they pass by me as the idle wind,*
> *Which I respect not.*

Shakespeare's *Julius Caesar*: Act IV, Scene II

Meanwhile, Anthony and Octavius Caesar, the dead Caesar's nephew and named successor, are leading a large army into Greece and have drawn up a list of Republican sympathizers to be killed. They then take their armies east to face Brutus and Cassius, who have managed to form their own armies as well.

Brutus considers his military options and recommends marching to meet the Caesarians at Phillipi, a key position in Macedonia. Cassius (more astute) disagrees with Brutus' strategy and prefers to hold back but once again loses the argument – worsted by the well-known advice that must have propelled many a hot-headed man into premature action:

> BRUTUS: *There is a tide in the affairs of men,*
> *Which, taken at the flood, leads on to fortune;*
> *Omitted, all the voyage of their life*
> *Is bound in shallows and in miseries.*
> *On such a full sea we are now afloat,*
> *And we must take the current when it serves,*
> *Or lose our ventures.*

Shakespeare's *Julius Caesar*: Act IV, Scene II

The two sides meet at Phillipi. Throughout the final Act of the play the freedom fighters are fighting on without hope. Cassius has become suspicious and has the premonition that he may not survive the battle. Brutus has similar misgivings because twice he has been visited by Caesar's ghost.

Brutus' impatience for battle brings disaster. The last remnant of justification ceases as the conspirators themselves acknowledge their error and fate. Facing certain defeat, both Cassius and Brutus ended up killing themselves with the same sword they had used to kill Caesar:

CASSIUS: Caesar; thou art revenged,
Even with the sword that kill'd thee.

BRUTUS: O Julius Caesar; thou art mighty yet!
Thy spirit walks abroad, and turns our swords
In our own proper entrails.

Shakespeare's *Julius Caesar*: Act V, Scene V

Because of his crime against established order, success will now go to the calculating and opportunistic Anthony who inherits the followers of Brutus and makes the final disposition; no matter he initiates no action but simply has to wait to gather the fallen fruit. In such a universe, one's chances of success are in direct proportion to one's skill in seizing his chances.

Shakespeare's *Julius Caesar* is the story of a political murder and a posthumous revenge; a thrilling and dramatic story where the victim of the murder turns into the soul of the revenge; and the murderer himself into the avenger's victim.

We witness the sudden fall of a man of overwhelming greatness and retribution falling upon the shoulders of an otherwise good man whose very goodness has rendered him wrong-headed in action.

What Shakespeare has done in this play is, as in others, to show the same penetration into political character and the wellsprings of public events as into those of everyday life. For example, the whole plot to liberate Rome fails as a direct result of the overgenerous and magnanimous character of Brutus and his overconfidence in the righteousness of his cause and an almost implicit trust in those around him.

Many commentators believe that Cassius should have been the leader of the conspiracy; instead, having organized it and seduced Brutus to give it the character of an honorable enterprise, he surrenders the leadership to Brutus; the politician plays second fiddle to the philosopher.

Had Cassius had his way with Anthony during the funeral speeches; or even at Phillipi, the story might have ended very differently. Brutus' idealism is admirable in and of itself; but a political enterprise such as this requires shrewd leadership.

Human history is not without its fair share of men who meant well themselves and thought well of others – only to fall prey to their security. It is as if the humanity and sincerity which dispose men to resist tyranny and injustice ironically render them unfit to cope with the cunning and power of those who are opposed to them.

Those who love freedom trust to the professions of others, because they are themselves sincere; they endeavour to secure the public good with the least possible hurt to its enemies who themselves have no regard to anything but their own selfish and unprincipled ends, and will stick at nothing to accomplish them.

Brutus is the only ethical and moral character in the entire play. Because of his thoroughly ethical cast of thought, many modern readers see the tragedy of Brutus in his rigid devotion to justice and fair play. He relentlessly pursues an ethical ideal which appears both naïve and incongruous in a universe of imperial glory, power, passionate love, envy and ambition.

As a Shakespearian commentator, Professor Chambers, has argued in "The Expression of Ideas, particularly Political Ideas in Shakespeare", *Julius Caesar* is an important work of art which focuses on a particular vision of life. The whole plot is unified and held together by an informing idea so that the interplay of the various characters contributes not solely to an evening's theatrical entertainment but also to a bold and imaginative statement about something of lasting importance and universal application.

It is against a background of politics that the play is cast and it has important lessons for us even in the XXI century; Shakespeare provides these lessons and presumably he intends that we take them. Shakespeare's *Julius Caesar* explores themes which were as relevant in the playwright's time as they are today; for example, it is heroic to seek freedom from corrupt power.

Moreover, Shakespeare presents us with the possibility of extracting certain general ideas from the play and debate them – either in the abstract or within the context of any given political situation anywhere in the world.

Julius Caesar is not only required reading for students of English literature but apparently for politicians as well. The February 16, 1996 by-election campaign in Central Castries provides an interesting case in point. Whether it was the partisan of St. Lucia's Julius Caesar, Neville Cenac, on the William Peter Boulevard; rebuking St. Lucia's Marcus Brutus, presumably for the latter's treachery towards his benefactor, Caesar, who had employed Brutus as St. Lucia's ambassador to the U.N: "*Ingratitude, more strong than traitor's arms....*" Or the Brutus partisan, Calixte George, on the Castries Market Steps; urging Brutus on to fight the by-election: "*There is a tide in the affairs of men....*"

CASSIUS: *Stoop then, and watch. How many ages hence*
           Shall this our lofty scene be acted over
           In states unborn and accents yet unknown!

Shakespeare's *Julius Caesar*: Act III, Scene I

PART III
ST. LUCIA'S JULIUS CAESAR

Perhaps, one of the least obvious, but nevertheless important, consequences of World War I, which broke out in 1914, was to accelerate the global revolution that forms so importantly a part of our time – the revolution against imperialism, or colonialism, as it is more commonly known.

At the turn of the 20th century, Great Britain, one of the bastions of colonialism, had an empire extending over 13,000,000 square miles, one quarter of the entire land mass of the earth, which was inhabited by 500,000,000 people, one quarter of the world population; and imposed its rule upon a large proportion of the teeming hordes of South-East Asia, India, the Middle East, Africa, Latin America and the Caribbean. France, the Netherlands, Belgium and Italy were lesser colonial powers.

The superior weaponry of the imperialists/colonialists inspired them to see themselves as a superior race with a God-given mission to carry the blessings of civilization to benighted natives of the "third world".

In some cases, the civilizing process was nothing more than a veneer of exploitation and impoverishment; though there were marginal benefits in the form of improved education and sanitation which redounded to the subjugated people. So long as the oppressed people saw little hope of changing their lot, they tolerated the rule of the European with no more than feeble protest.

However, World War I was a game changer; the fact of the great Christian powers killing each other on the battlefield made grim reality and destroyed their moral credibility.

World War I also facilitated the Bolshevik Revolution in 1917, and the triumph of communism in Russia and the propagation of its appeal to subjugated peoples to throw off their oppressors. Independence Movements among subject peoples gathered momentum and were now ready to burst into open revolt against colonialism as colonial citizens began to see the prospect of a better way of life than the cycle of famine, poverty, filth and disease.

In St. Lucia and the British West Indies, as they were then called, after much agitation for constitutional advancement and self-determination, elections for a Legislative Council were held in 1924 under a limited franchise which still left elected members in the minority. Nominated members appointed by the colonial Governor or Administrator still dominated.

The cries of the people for full representation were ignored. Freedom would, however, not be achieved without struggle. The 1930s was perhaps the most tumultuous decade in the history of the West Indies; engulfed as they were with strikes, riots and violence. In some cases, the British Government had to send in the marines to cool off the heat.

The protests were geared towards the alleviation of the economic, social and political plight of the working classes – the most direct victims of colonial exploitation – demanding among other things, better working conditions, better education, an end to poverty and squalor, and an end to colonialism itself.

In 1937, the British Government appointed a Royal Commission under the chairmanship of Lord Moyne to investigate the causes of the widespread workers' rebellion. The Commission's Report was a damning indictment on the way the British colonies were being governed and administered. It found fault with nearly every aspect of British policy towards the colonies – education, health care, housing, labour relations and economic matters generally were all condemned. "...The situation of the poor offers admirable opportunity for social reform," the Report concluded.

The Moyne Commission also stated that the claims for full representation were warranted to give the islanders a greater voice in their own affairs; pointing further that the growing political consciousness was sufficiently widespread to make it doubtful whether any reform, social or otherwise, would be completely successful unless accompanied by the greatest of constitutional development.

The Moyne Report resulted in the passage of the Colonial Development and Welfare Act of 1940, which provided aid to improve the economic and social conditions of the islands. It also resulted in a succession of constitutional reforms: the most important of which was the granting of Adult Suffrage in 1951; the partial introduction of the ministerial system in 1956; the full introduction of the ministerial system in 1960; associated statehood status in 1967; and political independence in 1979.

The political party system in the Caribbean, like the trade union movement, emerged out of the struggles of the 1930s; as colonial citizens, still fighting off the shackles of slavery abolished since 1834, sought to take the movement toward political and economic freedom one step further by targeting voting and labour rights.

Caribbean nationalism was, accordingly, born of the need to create societies founded in freedom. Similarly, Caribbean politics proceeded on the assumption that freedom must open the doors to social justice. Alexander Bustamente of Jamaica, Uriah Butler of Trinidad & Tobago, Clement Payne of Barbados and T.A. Maryshaw of Grenada were foremost among those who threw down the gauntlet on behalf of the working classes in the pioneering decade of the 1930s.

Here in St. Lucia, George Charles, Martin Jn. Baptiste, Charles Augustin among others were later to challenge the status quo by issuing the demand for political self-determination as they commenced to fashion the political organization that would first win and later manage colonial change.

The St. Lucia Labour Party (SLP) was founded in October of 1950 as the political arm of the Labour Movement. The vehicle for the transfer of power and influence was Adult Suffrage which was won in 1951; and which opened the doors to full representative Government.

The Labour Movement had both a social and an economic component; both of which aimed to break the embrace between the colonial Government and the landowning plantocracy. The model of society was "us" and "them"; "us", being the landowning plantocracy and "them", being the new mass society ushered in by universal Adult Suffrage – the right of every man to vote.

General elections were held for the first time in St. Lucia in 1951, under the new constitutional requirements of Adult Suffrage. The St. Lucia Labour Party was opposed by the People's Progressive Party (PPP); which was also organized in 1950 to champion the interests of the upper classes. The SLP captured 5 of the 8 seats.

The revolution of the 1930s did not remain intact for very long as the 1960s witnessed a counter-revolution of sorts as the anti-colonial movement became subverted and shunted to a side by the conservatively educated class that was now returning home from Great Britain; most notably, in Barbados, Clement Payne was replaced by Grantley Adams; in Trinidad & Tobago, Uriah Butler was superseded by Eric Williams; and in St. Lucia, George Charles was supplanted by St. Lucia's Julius Caesar.

In 1954, St. Lucia's Julius Caesar and his close associate, Maurice Mason, arrived in St. Lucia from the United Kingdom after pursuing qualifications in law. On their return home, they wasted no time in identifying with the working-class struggle by joining the two main organs of the Labour Movement, the St. Lucia Workers' Union and the St. Lucia Labour Party. The Labour Movement heralded this youthful and professional injection of new blood with much gusto and enthusiasm and quickly embraced them into their leadership.

The second general elections were held in 1954 under the then mandatory 3-year term. The St. Lucia Labour Party was to receive the first blast of our Caesar's vaulting ambition when it came to the nomination of candidates for the elections as he insisted on having himself nominated for the Dennery & Micoud constituency; notwithstanding the fact that the SLP had already nominated James Charles, who was the SLP incumbent. In the event, our Caesar "crossed the Rubicon" and easily captured the seat for himself as "Independent Labour".

The St. Lucia Labour Party retained its 3-seat majority in the 1954 elections; however, it lost 2 of its incumbents, including Caesar's casualty – the said James Charles.

There was a further constitutional advance on March 1, 1956 with the introduction of partial ministerial Government; heralding the first St. Lucia Labour Party Government of St. Lucia. For the first time, elected members dominated both the Executive and Legislative Councils with the Executive as a full-fledged policy-making body. Three ministerial departments were created: Trade and Industry, Communications and Works, and Social Affairs.

But even given this new constitutional development, the Governor of the Windward Islands still continued to wield great power and influence; most notably, retaining control over the island's Finances, the Audit Department, Internal Security, Defence, Immigration and External Affairs. Heads of Government departments were free to disagree with Ministers' directives and have the matter adjudicated upon by the Governor. Even proposed legislation emanating from the Executive Council had to be endorsed by the Colonial Office in London.

Crown colony rule was hard to jettison and a source of great frustration for reform-minded Ministers.

After the social, political and economic improvements resulting from the Moyne Commission, St. Lucia still had economic problems. The price of sugar, the main export crop, had started to fluctuate on the world market and a foreign-exchange crisis loomed large on the horizon – the island could not earn enough from sugar to pay for all the things it needed from overseas.

Also looming ominously largely on the horizon was the sugar beet plant; Europe had begun to produce its own sugar from sugar beet and did not need the island's sugar anymore. It was at this juncture that the British Government realized that the islands needed a new export crop.

Enter bananas. The banana plant was chosen as the natural choice for the Windward Islands because of their fertile soil and mountainous terrain, which suited the cultivation of this crop.

In 1953, Geest, a British company, was awarded a contract to buy all the bananas grown in the Windward Islands. At the same time, London imposed a tariff on all bananas coming into Britain from other countries to guarantee the Windward Islands a protected market for their bananas.

The banana industry soon mushroomed to become the island's biggest money spinner; the "green gold", as it was called, produced an aura of immediate and potential prosperity. An army of small growers were assisted with subsidized fertilizer and other farming necessities. There was a strong marketing institution in place and a programme for the construction of a network of feeder roads to underpin the island's future development.

In all this period of apparent prosperity, the sugar industry remained problem-plagued. By the mid-1950s, the owners of the Cul-de-Sac and Roseau Estates cultivating sugar cane for the manufacture of sugar had concluded that they could no longer continue operations due to the falling price of sugar on the world market.

By that time too, the sugar industry had also become a plaything of politics and ambitious politicians. In the sugar crop of 1957, the opportunity presented itself during a political "wild cat strike" which started at Roseau and quickly spread to Cul-de-Sac, to Crown Lands, and to the Dennery Estates and Factories (comprising the entire sugar belt), in demand for increased wages for all daily paid, task, and factory workers.

The principal instigators of the strike were George Charles, Martin Jn. Baptiste and St. Lucia's Julius Caesar.

On the first morning of the strike, Caesar and the other strike leaders called the workers at Roseau and Cul-de-Sac off their jobs and proceeded to Crown Lands and the Dennery Estates to spread the flames – although the owner of the Dennery Estates and Factories, Dennis Barnard, a white planter, apparently did not take the threat seriously on the mistaken belief that his loyal workers would not obey the strike call.

After all the workers at the Dennery Estates and Factories had disloyally walked out in support of the strike, Caesar walked inside the factory in a show of bravado when an irate Dennis Barnard arrived on the scene and told him in insulting language to get off his property. A brief confrontation that involved the mutual reaching for revolvers ensued but the situation was calmed down:

CAESAR: *Cowards die many times before their deaths;*
The valiant never tastes of death but once.
Of all the wonders that I yet have heard,
It seems to me most strange that men should fear;
Seeing that death, a necessary end,
Will come when it will come.

Shakespeare's *Julius Caesar:* Act III, Scene I

By the third week of the strike, several war ships had berthed in the Castries harbour, as if to crush a rebellion. When George Charles, in his capacity as a Minister of Government, sought to inquire of the Governor as to the business of the war ships – what with the fact that there was no sign of open hostility, save for Caesar's derailment of a few wagons under his "operation roadblock" – the Minister was informed that he could not be privy to the actions of the Governor because of his leadership in the strike.

On the Wednesday of the third week of the strike, while attending mediation talks between the parties and the Labour Commissioner, Ira Simmons, Charles received information that a large number of sugar workers from the Cul-de-Sac Valleys were marching on Castries to make their presence felt at the mediation talks; whereupon Charles and Caesar immediately left the meeting to meet the advancing army of striking sugar cane workers.

From Charles' own personal account, they were about half way up Bridge Street when they were intercepted by armed police in battle gear and hustled out of their car. Castries had been placed under a state of emergency by the proclamation of the Governor; there was a heavy police presence in full battle regalia. When Charles and Caesar decided to abandon their car to the police and walk to meet the workers, there resulted a fracas between Charles and the police that almost cost the former his life. If it wasn't for Caesar's quick reaction who pushed Charles away, the latter might well have found himself at the business end of a police bayonet.

The effect of the police harassment was to abort the mission to meet the striking workers who had themselves been bundled up and thrown into police trucks and taken to police headquarters in the midst of police military battle cries.

The strike ended after 6 weeks of bitter struggle after increasing battle fatigue. The terms of the settlement were conveyed to the workers by the unionists via a series of meetings in the sugar belt.

The struggle of the workers might have come to an end, not so the struggle of the union leaders who still had to face arrest, fine and imprisonment. For his part, St. Lucia's Julius Caesar was hauled before the Dennery District Court on a series of charges arising out of the strike, including setting up roadblocks.

The union mobilized busloads of its members and supporters from the sugar belt and Castries in a show of solidarity by trade-union leaders headed by George Charles and Martin Jn. Baptiste. St. Lucia's Julius Caesar was variously convicted and fined by Magistrate Hercules.

Thus, during a recent May Day rally, St. Lucia's Julius Caesar would recall the days when he had to stand in the dock "like a common criminal" because of his efforts to "break the back of the plantocracy...."

Our Caesar's histrionics in the sugar valleys deeply impressed the working classes as his personality became transformed into that of an icon. He had broken the credibility barrier and was the right man in the right place at the right time. Some even dubbed him "Daddy Compton".

In the aftermath of the 6-week strike, Caesar, who had been shunned and alienated by the St. Lucia Labour Party for defying the party in the 1954 elections, was reprieved and returned to the fold of the Labour Movement. His committed involvement in the strike at the risk of both life and limb had impressed many in the Labour Movement and cultivated a new and deep sense of brotherhood.

In the period between the elections and the strike, apart from attending meetings of the Legislative Council, Caesar's political activities had been confined to writing a biting column in the journal of the Labour Movement "The Worker's Clarion" called "JACK SPANIARD" in which he made his attacks on the plantocracy and social discrimination. He also used this column to get even with those he thought had unfairly left him out of the choice of Ministers in 1956.

It was time to prepare for the 1957 general elections. At the SLP convention of that year a new constitution was adopted which for the first time made provision for a political leader and a deputy political leader. The inaugural constitution of the party in 1950 had only provided for a chairman, which post was held by Allen Lewis. George Charles was elected political leader and

Caesar, deputy political leader. The Labour Party also chose the star as its symbol; hitherto it had been the teacup.

The 1957 general elections were quite predictable; the SLP won a landslide victory – 7 out of 8. Caesar's ministerial ambition was realized; he was brought into the Cabinet as Minister of Trade and Industry.

In 1959, the British Government convened a conference of representatives of the Governments of the Windward and Leeward Islands to discuss a formula for further change in the 1956 constitution. The result was the 1959 constitution which for the first time made provision for a Chief Minister to which the political leader of the SLP, George Charles, fitted. He was sworn in on January 1, 1960.

For St. Lucia, it was another general election in 1961 – one year and several months before the 5-year term which had been introduced in 1957 was due to expire. The early poll was in keeping with a commitment to call general elections within 1 year of the introduction of the 1959 constitution.

An Electoral Boundaries Commission was appointed by the SLP Government which recommended that St. Lucia be divided into 10 constituencies instead of 8. As a result Dennery and Micoud became disjointed and North Castries (which included Gros Islet) was divided into two constituencies to create a new constituency of North-East Castries.

The St. Lucia Labour Party wasted no time in setting its election machinery in motion and appealed to the electorate for a clean sweep of the polls on the premise of the performance of the Labour Government. In the result the Government won all but 1 seat; that of the PPP's George Mallet in Central Castries.

The newly created position of Chief Minister soon set personal ambitions in motion for leadership and control. At the convention of the St. Lucia Labour Party before the 1961 general elections, there was an unsuccessful attempt by Caesar to overthrow George Charles as political leader of the SLP in favour of himself.

This power play created some doubt as to who would be the Chief Minister following the 1961 general elections; what with the fact that the constitution required that in the appointment of a Chief Minister, the Governor must consult with elected members in order to determine the elected member who would be most likely to command the confidence of the majority of elected members in the House of Assembly. This could have been either SLP's political leader or his deputy political leader, St. Lucia's Julius Caesar.

In the final analysis, 4 members of Caesar's disgruntled faction wrote to the Governor to state their preference. However, by the time the Governor's mandatory consultation with elected members had been completed, it was George Charles and not Caesar who was summoned to Government House to be appointed Chief Minister; 6 elected members had recommended Charles' re-appointment – including the lone PPP member, George Mallet.

Our Caesar took this as a slap in the face and declined an invitation to continue to serve in the Cabinet. Moreover, at the first sitting of the House of Assembly following the 1961 general elections he withdrew his seat from the Government benches to the Opposition; along with his lieutenants, Maurice Mason and Vincent Monrose – shrinking the Labour Government's majority to a precarious one with which to implement the promises of its 1961 manifesto.

As George Charles, in his last years, was later to lament: "Perhaps all sores may have been healed because of the strong friendship which existed between leaders of the party; but history has taught us the insatiable desire of immediate ambition. Indeed, there was time for fulfilling reasonable ambitions because of the years' gap between [Julius Caesar] and myself. Any figment of such hope was destroyed when the dissenting faction of [Julius Caesar], Maurice Mason and Dr. Vincent Monrose formed a new party which they called the National Labour Movement with the precise intention of opposing the St. Lucia Labour Party."

The new Labour Party Government had barely been announced in 1961 when Caesar's faction, supported by the People's Progressive Party, petitioned the High Court to ask the Court to declare the 1961 general election results null and void on the ground that "the elections supervisor had produced the wrong form for the signature of candidates".

The petition went before Judge Chanery for adjudication. Apprehensive about the implications of the petition, the new Government consulted the Legal Department of the British Government in London on the substance of the application and got the assurance that the petition could not alter the expressed wishes of the St. Lucian electorate.

However, C.M. Charles did not rest content with the opinion of the Legal Department and extracted an undertaking from London that in the event that the petition was granted it would be set aside by a validating Order in Council.

Judge Chanery ruled in favour of the petition but the validating Order in Council saved the new Labour Government.

Caesar's faction, aided and abetted by the PPP, having failed in its intentions, initiated a series of public meetings to protest what it called interference by the Government in the judiciary. It even threatened to hold one of the meetings directly outside the residence of the Chief Minister. There were also nightly candlelit demonstrations to Government House, the Governor's residence.

Our Caesar's efforts to overthrow the Labour Government by petition and by political pressure generally having failed thus far, the St. Lucia Banana Growers Association (SLBGA) looked like a soft target for economic sabotage and destabilization; especially as many of those who had now defected from the SLP were influential members of the SLBGA.

Following persistent reports of corruption and inefficiency in the banana industry, the Labour Government moved to restructure the SLBGA by passing legislation to remove politicians from the board of the SLBGA. Further, it sought assistance from the U.K.

Government to provide expert advice to ensure the stability of the industry.

On April 1, 1964, in a plot with Caesar to cease power, J.M.D. Bousquet and his brother Allan Bousquet, resigned from the Labour Government; citing their dissatisfaction with the Labour Government for what they called its interference with the SLBGA.

For many St. Lucians this was a blatant act of betrayal by the Bousquet brothers as the Government had now lost its majority and had to go back to the polls on June 25, 1964. In order to fight the early poll, the National Labour Movement merged with the People's Progressive Party to form the United Workers' Party (UWP) under the leadership of St. Lucia's Julius Caesar. George Charles was defeated by a majority of 8-2 by Caesar.

PART IV
ST. LUCIA'S MARCUS BRUTUS

With the advent of the 1970s, St. Lucia's Marcus Brutus stole the stage as far as populism was concerned. He stood for what he and his audience took to be enduring values. His mission was to activate the soul, to bring the critical spirit to political and social consciousness.

Brutus' vision invoked the language of awe; a cogent and infectious message from outside that time and beyond its unprincipled and self-serving pragmatism. He almost single-handedly pioneered the popular education of the masses with his political rhetoric; moving across the country like a man possessed by an entire truth, needing only to repeat it endlessly.

The message contained an entire gospel of human and social values. He would address his audience in a dark, deep voice – rich in gravity and suffering. Unlike Caesar, Brutus was a painstakingly strategic politician; his message was geared towards long-term reform rather than quick fixes.

But the simplicity of the message was its strength and its delivery – that blend of severity and warmth that made Brutus probably the island's single most loved politician.

In 1974, an election year, the St. Lucia Labour Action Movement (SLAM) under the leadership of Brutus merged with the St. Lucia Labour Party – whose internecine factionalism since losing power to Caesar in 1964 had consigned it to the limbo of hopeless oppositionism – with our Brutus as its de facto leader. The revolution of the 1970s was launched.

The merger meant that life would never be the same again for our Caesar (who had now assumed the title of Premier as a result of a further constitutional advance that rendered St. Lucia, and the other Windward and Leeward Islands, an "associated state" with Great Britain with the former responsible for its own internal affairs and Great Britain still responsible for its external affairs and defence).

Since his accession to ultimate power in 1964, Caesar had used Machiavellian tactics to divide and rule St. Lucia. With Brutus now hard on his heels, the Premier responded by making sweeping changes to the electoral boundaries; he gerrymandered 17 out of 10 seats. He had hoped for a landslide victory; but the result was a cliffhanger.

On the night of the 1974 elections the results were fed into the House of Assembly, turned election headquarters, but up to 11:15 p.m., no clear lead had emerged and it could have been either our Caesar or our Brutus to rule and control St. Lucia for the next 5 years.

At 6:26 p.m., one of the 6 telephones installed at the makeshift election headquarters went off; suddenly, there was an air of expectancy. Alas, it was a false alarm; it was a wrong number that was dialed. 2 minutes later, a call came from the constituency of South Castries but it was cut off.

The first genuine call came from a polling station in the constituency of South-East Castries – the battleground where Brutus was being challenged by lone female candidate, Heraldine Rock of Caesar's UWP. Out of a total number of 265 votes cast in that polling station, Brutus polled 127 to Rock's 128. Rock's early lead was, however, short-lived; another call from the same constituency gave 61 to Brutus and Rock 41.

This pattern of fluctuating leads for candidates was the order of the night; leaving announcers and reporters on tenterhooks. The big question was: Would there be a change of Government or would Caesar hold on to power?

At 6:40 p.m., there was a rumour spreading like wild fire that Gregor Mason of the SLP had defeated Caesar's man in the Gros Islet constituency by a landslide; even though not one polling station there had reported in.

10 minutes later, a downpour started as newsmen looked outside at the gloomy, darkening skies; hunkering down on their haunches for the long, hard night ahead.

The first conclusive result came at 7:05 p.m. from the constituency of South Castries; Jon Odlum, Brutus' unexceptionable younger brother, had soundly beaten Caesar's man, lawyer, Primrose Bledman – Brutus' party drawing first blood.

At this juncture, a deluge of results started pouring in; Caesar's man in the North Dennery constituency, Dr. Vincent Monrose, had captured that seat to level the score.

The next result came in from Central Castries; Caesar's deputy political leader, George Mallet, retained his seat – polling more votes than SLP and Independent candidates put together.

It was now 2 to 1 in favour of the UWP. The next result was phoned in from South Dennery; lawyer, Clendon Mason, of the UWP had captured that seat; placing the UWP in a 3 to 1 position.

The lead was cut down to 3 to 2 when Peter Josie of the SLP captured the Marchand seat. The election could go any way now.

UWP got a further boost when Allan Bousquet brought the North-East Castries seat home to the ruling party; giving Caesar a comfortable margin of 4 to 2.

It was now 8:30 p.m., and the rain had stopped; but outside election headquarters the city of Castries looked like a ghost town

– completely deserted. There was as yet no sign of revelry from either party and it painted a pretty solemn picture.

Allan Louisy easily took the Laborie seat to move the SLP closer to the finish line: 9 out of 17 would be the majority. It was now 4 to 3 and the tension inside election headquarters was simply unbearable.

Christopher Alcindor brought new hope to the UWP when he carried the Soufriere seat home; bringing the score to 5 to 3, with the UWP in the lead. It could still be anybody's election; it could be either Brutus' or Caesar's.

The surprise victory of legendary criminal lawyer, Kenneth Foster, in Anse-La-Raye/Canaries for Brutus' party made the result of the election even more uncertain; pushing the score to 5 to 4 at 9: 50 p.m.

By 10:10 p.m., the tension had reached near fever pitch; what with the marginal victory of SLP's Bruce Williams over UWP chairman, formidable lawyer Henry Giraudy, by only 2 votes in South Vieux Fort. The tension was not helped by the fact that Giraudy was adamant that 3 of his rejected votes should be counted; hinting at a possible Court challenge. The score was now 5 to 5.

At 10:15 p.m., shock news was phoned into election headquarters: Heraldine Rock had heralded the unlikely defeat of Brutus on behalf of Caesar. Now the score stood at 6 to 5 in favour of the UWP – but it could also be 7 to 4, depending on the final determination of South Vieux Fort.

From North-West Castries news came that Hollis Bristol had carried that seat for the UWP; giving his party a critical 7 to 5 advantage. Two more seats for the UWP would seal the deal for Caesar; but those two seats did not come easily.

The next result came in from Gros Islet; confirming the earlier rumour that SLP had won the seat by a landslide. The constantly shifting result now stood at 7 to 6. With only 4 more seats to be accounted for, pandemonium broke out at election headquarters.

Caesar's supporters received a well-needed bit of heartening news when it was announced that Rodney Jn. Baptiste had carried home the North Micoud seat for Caesar. Now it stood at 8 to 6 – 1 more seat and Caesar would remain in power.

Brutus' supporters got a heartening piece of news when it was confirmed the Boswell Williams carried home the North Vieux Fort seat for the SLP.

It was now 8 to 7 in favour of the UWP with only 2 more seats to be accounted for and upon which the fate of St. Lucia rested for the next 5 years. What happened to Caesar himself in his battleground in South Micoud? Did Brutus' fighters there defeat him? Newsmen remained sat on the edge of their seats.

At 11:40 p.m., news was phoned into election headquarters that Caesar had actually crushed his opponent in his constituency – giving Caesar control over St. Lucia for another 5 years.

However, there was still 1 more seat that had not sent in its tally, the Choiseul constituency. Frantic calls to the police station revealed that lawyer Evans Calderon of the SLP had soundly defeated the UWP's J.M.D. Bousquet; giving Caesar but an uncomfortable and precarious majority of 9 to 8.

When the electoral history of St. Lucia is written, the 1974 general elections would probably go down as St. Lucia's most historic – and not without good reason; it was the first time that the electoral map was divided into 17 constituencies, hitherto it was 10; it was the first time that voters could vote at 18, hitherto it was 21; it was the first time that an Opposition party went to the polls with no clearly defined political leader but a conglomerate of 4 violently deferring political personalities as potential Premier: Brutus, Allan Louisy, Kenneth Foster and Hunter François.

But by far, the most significant consequence of the 1974 elections, in terms of the future leadership and direction of St. Lucia, was the defeat of Brutus by Caesar's Rock.

When it was confirmed at 10:15 p.m. on the election night of Monday May 6, 1974, that Caesar's Rock had stopped Brutus in his tracks, it might well have been the rock of destiny which had buffeted Brutus.

For had Brutus defeated Rock, he would almost certainly have become in 1974 the undisputed leader of the Opposition St. Lucia Labour Party; destined to become Prime Minister in 1979.

The destiny of St. Lucia's Marcus Brutus was well and truly sealed on the night of Monday May 6, 1974, at 10:15 p.m. as a political loser:

> *BRUTUS:*   *There is a tide in the affairs of men,*
>   *Which, taken at the flood, leads on to fortune;*
>   *Omitted, all the voyage of their life*
>   *Is bound in shallows and in miseries.*
>   *On such a full sea we are now afloat,*
>   *And we must take the current when it serves,*
>   *Or lose our ventures.*

Shakespeare's *Julius Caesar*: Act IV, Scene II

So our Brutus missed the boat. As karma would have it, the hapless Allan Louisy, who won a seat in the election went on to become the de jure political leader of the St. Lucia Labour Party and Prime Minister of St. Lucia on July 2, 1979, much to the chagrin of our Brutus; and thereby setting the stage for the bitter and ultimately suicidal "Quarrel Scene" or power struggle that, to all intents and purposes, eventually put paid to the political careers of both men.

As Brutus himself put it following the historic election: "In my fight were amassed all the forces in this country. I won't call them forces of reaction, I will say people with entrenched interests; the whole establishment brought all its weight against me in a desperate effort to prevent me from getting into the House of Assembly. This was not something I realized around the time of the election. In addition to that, there were other forces in the election which proved too much for me."

But the knife-edge result left Caesar with little elbow room. Indeed, Caesar might have been declared the "winner" under our arcane electoral laws but not a winner in any real political sense. First and foremost, he had failed to get the two-thirds majority he wanted in order to augment his growing power and influence; instead, he was handed a shoestring majority of only 1 seat (leaving to a side the political chicanery that took place in South Vieux Fort the morning after the election to give him a majority of 10 to 7).

Caesar was only able to hold on to power based on the premise of his Government's modest performance. Moreover, Caesar's campaign was underwritten by strong financial support, especially from merchants in the private sector. Caesar's victory was, therefore, a pyrrhic victory.

The St. Lucia Labour Party did very well in 1974; a fact that, by his own admission, even surprised Caesar. It was not only a moral victory but, in many ways, a political victory as well for the SLP. The stage for the 1979 electoral fight was set!

But the St. Lucian electorate also acquitted well of itself; demonstrating as it did its political savvy and intellectualism; it returned Caesar's Government, albeit with decreasing enthusiasm, which had performed competently in office, if not inspiringly. But the electorate also sent to the House of Assembly a strong Opposition, which had been sadly lacking for some time.

Prior to the advent of Brutus in 1974, the SLP Opposition was no match for Caesar; a timid and torpid Opposition that had only known struggle headed by a ragbag of non-entities whose favourite subject at school must have been long division as they allowed Caesar to divide and rule St. Lucia.

With its long history of internecine civil war, the SLP's power potential was anything but auspicious. Its image was, at best, pathetic; and, at worst, unacceptable as a viable alternative to St. Lucia's Julius Caesar. Whereas most Labour Parties elsewhere were strong, united and did well at elections, the St. Lucia Labour Party, before the arrival of Brutus, was weak, divided and nadir.

Somehow, it lacked a certain charisma; somehow, the ground seemed dour.

By the late 1970s, a wind of change was sweeping across the Caribbean and revolution seemed everywhere. In neighbouring Dominica and Grenada, people's heroes, now turned dictators, Patrick John and Eric Gairy respectively, were being unceremoniously catapulted out of power by angry, popular, people's uprisings.

There was talk of the domino theory, which had it that it was only a matter of time for St. Lucia and the other islands to go the revolutionary way; especially as implicit in Brutus' platform rhetoric was the possibility of a violent takeover.

The air of a revolution only served to fuel Caesar's increasingly paranoid sense of encirclement. He moved to tighten the provisions of the Public Order Act in a dictatorial move to stifle public dissent, rising now to a dangerous pith, in a desperate bid to hold on to power. He introduced new unconstitutional laws to restrict freedom of speech, of expression and of assembly; conveniently forgetting his activities in the sugar belt in the 1950s:

> BRUTUS: *But 'tis common proof*
> *That lowliness is young ambition's ladder,*
> *Whereto the climber-upward turns his face;*
> *But when he once attains the upmost rung,*
> *He then unto the ladder turns his back,*
> *Looks in the clouds, scorning the base degrees*
> *By which he did ascend.*

Shakespeare's *Julius Caesar*: Act II, Scene I

THE PEOPLE TAKE

TO THE STREETS

The late 1970s too was a time when the 1960s' revolutionary movement in America called "black power" was starting to take its toll on Caribbean politics. There was widespread discontent with the made-in-England model of Government known as the "Westminster system". As far as the radicals of the time, including Brutus, were concerned; Fidel Castro was God, Cuba was heaven, and socialism, the only way to heaven.

In St. Lucia, many people saw Brutus as St. Lucia's answer to Fidel Castro.

The situation on the ground in St. Lucia was getting increasingly explosive; which, of course, did not help Caesar's nerves; sitting as he was on a knife-edge majority in Parliament.

Instigated chiefly by Brutus, public servants began a rising tide of protest against Caesar; clamouring for, among other things, retroactive pay due them by Caesar. But Caesar remained defiant, even in the face of widespread industrial action and strikes that almost crippled the economic life of the country: "You can put a gun to my head, I will not pay," was Caesar's stern refrain.

Brutus under police arrest in Castries

Inch by inch, as each of his wile manoeuvres rebounded on him, Caesar was being forced into a corner. But those who urged Caesar to give in to public pressure in the national interest were disappointed. Instead, the Premier unleashed the dreaded Special Services Unit of the police force (SSU, Caesar's agents of tyranny, armed to the teeth with sophisticated American military hardware) on protestors and dissenters while the Premier and his wife, Janice Compton, arrogantly flew first class to London to see the movie premier of "Fire Power" – a low-budget film that was shot, in part, in St. Lucia.

By 1978, Caesar had made up his mind to take St. Lucia to full political independence from Britain in order to augment his regal powers. Despite public concern about his indecent haste, he flatly refused to submit his idea to a referendum or an election as a precondition, as demanded by Brutus and his followers. There was scant public consultation on the not insignificant matter of St. Lucia's political independence; let alone public approval. Caesar's self-sufficient arrogance had become simply breathtaking. Pronouncements such as "Shut up and listen to your masters" had become the order of the day.

But history was on Caesar's side with his independence obsession – if not the people of St. Lucia. For it was a time when the imperialist "mother country" itself, Great Britain, was too preoccupied with its own domestic woes to care to keep impoverished colonies and protectorates. Not only was Caesar's St. Lucia crippled by strikes and discontent, Jim Callaghan's Britain was also itself crippled and virtually broken down by the infamous "winter of discontent" strikes; with the IMF having to be called in to rescue the less-than-incompetent Labour Government of Jim Callaghan.

And so, shortly after midnight on the morning of February 22, 1979, the crown colony of St. Lucia of 130,000 people severed its ties with its mother country to become a full-fledged independent country. Caesar became the Prime Minister of St. Lucia and secured his place in history as the "father of the nation".

> CASSIUS: *Upon what meat doth this our Caesar feed,*
> *That he is grown so great?*
> *The fault, dear Brutus, is not in our stars,*
> *But in ourselves, that we are underlings.*

Shakespeare's *Julius Caesar*: Act I, Scene III

But political independence in and of itself was not enough to save Caesar from a humiliating defeat at the polls principally at the hands of Brutus some 4 months thereafter on July 2, 1979.

"The St. Lucia Labour Party did not win the elections. They hijacked the country!" Caesar cried, his eyes glistening with tears and flickering with incomprehension at what he perceived as ingratitude. However, few people shed any tears for Caesar. Indeed, the entire country heaved a huge sigh of relief. The general feeling was something like "Good Riddance":

> ANTHONY: *This was the most unkindest cut of all,*
> *For when the noble Caesar saw him stab,*
> *Ingratitude, more strong than traitor's arms,*
> *Quite vanquished him: then burst his mighty heart;*
> *And, in his mantle muffling up his face,*
> *Even at the base of Pompey's statua,*
> *Which all the while ran blood, great Caesar fell.*
> *O! what a fall was there, my countrymen.*

Shakespeare's *Julius Caesar*: Act III, Scene II

> CINNA: *Liberty! Freedom! Tyranny is dead!*
> *Run hence, proclaim, cry it about the streets.*

> BRUTUS: *Let's all cry "Peace, Freedom, and Liberty!"*

CASSIUS: Some to the common pulpits, and cry out:
Liberty! Freedom! and Enfranchisement!
So oft as that shall be,
So oft shall the knot of us be call'd
The men that gave their country LIBERTY!

Shakespeare's *Julius Caesar*: Act III, Scene I

St. Lucia's Marcus Brutus virtually embodied the SLP vision that finally put paid to St. Lucia's Julius Caesar in 1979; incarnating as he did, the hopes and dreams of ordinary St. Lucians, whom he liked to refer to as "the masses".

His attractiveness cut right across party lines. He had the makings of a good two-way bet; militancy to mobilize the partisans, and charisma to inspire the rest.

Niccolo Machiavelli, the Italian political philosopher, once wrote: "Men are fond of novelty. So much so that those who are prosperous desire it as much as those who are poor. For in prosperity, men get fed up; and in adversity, they get cast down."

Our Brutus represented an entrancing new identity for St. Lucia and added to local politics that which had been lacking for umpteen years; a new zest, a new impulse. Hence his attractiveness across the board:

Probably the most significant thing one may say about this hero as an admirable character is that, however difficult it is to probe the meaning of his tragedy, it is not at all difficult to understand the hold his humanity has upon us. When he arouses our admiration he does not leave us uncertain why he does so. Moreover, he arouses some measure of admiration in all of us. He does not create among us a camp of condemners as well as a camp of praisers; for he is a noble spirit in the simple sense of the word. If good and evil are mighty opposites in the finite universe, as Shakespeare often makes them in his tragedies, then Brutus can be placed on the side of good without debate and without involved justification. He has plainly a bent toward good. Brutus has a consuming desire to further the cause of right.

Williard Farnhan: Shakespeare's Tragic Frontier – High-Minded Heroes (1950)

So the St. Lucia Labour Party returned to power in 1979 after it had been defeated by Caesar in 1964. It was Brutus who had underpinned the 1979 SLP mass appeal with his articulation of a new vision of Government which was really the intellectual expression of the ordinary man's dreams and aspirations. He gave facility to the ideas and concerns of a disgruntled people who had been for 15 years before led into paralysis and drift by Caesar's self-serving and visionless leadership.

But even though the impression had grown that Brutus personified the hopes and dreams of ordinary St. Lucians, the reality, however, was less romantic. Brutus had promised "peace, freedom and liberty" (Act III, Scene I) but peace, freedom and liberty came there none. After all, Brutus was too busy in Government fighting to wrest power from Prime Minister Allan Louisy in the "Quarrel Scene". Cast by events in that role, Brutus fumbled and flunked it:

The Quarrel Scene shows how low the tone of Cassius has fallen since he has dealt with the assassination as a political weapon; and even Brutus' moderation has hardened into unpleasing harshness. We get a supernatural foreshadowing of the end in the appearance to Brutus of Caesar's ghost. This lends the authority of the invisible to our sense that the conspirators' cause is doomed.

R.G. Moulton: Shakespeare as a Dramatic Artiste (1885)

Not unlike the audience in Shakespeare's *Julius Caesar*, the leadership "Quarrel" between Brutus and Louisy on the Labour Party stage gave the local political audience "a supernatural foreshadowing of the end" and the imminent appearance of Caesar's ghost:

ANTHONY: Caesar's spirit, raging for revenge,
With Ate by his side, come hot from hell,
Shall in these confines, with a Monarch's voice
Cry "Havoc!" and let slip the dogs of war.

Shakespeare's *Julius Caesar*: Act III, Scene I

Indeed, within less than 3 years, by the middle of 1982, Caesar's ghost had exacted its revenge on the "foolish virgins" who had masterminded his political assassination; killing themselves with the same sword they had used to kill Caesar:

CASSIUS: Caesar; thou art revenged,
Even with the sword that kill'd thee.

BRUTUS: O Julius Caesar; thou art mighty yet!
Thy spirit walks abroad, and turns our swords
In our own proper entrails.

Shakespeare's *Julius Caesar*: Act V, Scene V

Our Brutus – no doubt, worsted by the celebrated advice that must have propelled many hot-blooded people into premature action – reached for the stars and fell into the sea:

BRUTUS: There is a tide in the affairs of men,
Which, taken at the flood, leads on to fortune;
Omitted, all the voyage of their life
Is bound in shallows and in miseries.
On such a full sea we are now afloat,

> *And we must take the current when it serves,*
> *Or lose our ventures.*

Shakespeare's *Julius Caesar*: Act IV, Scene II

Brutus at Bristol University

St. Lucia's Marcus Brutus was born on June 24, 1934; the son of a large Castries family of 11 with modest means. His father was a conscientious city barber. Brutus attended the Methodist

School and St. Mary's College where he distinguished himself as a sportsman as well as a man of letters before he proceeded to the United Kingdom to pursue higher studies. After a year at the North-Western Polytechnic in London he entered the University of Bristol to pursue a degree course in English literature. He spent 3 years at Bristol where he made history by being the first negro ever to fill the post of President of the 5,000-strong University of Bristol Students' Union because of his remarkable debating skills. He represented Bristol University in the National Debating Competition involving the students of all the Universities in the United Kingdom.

Union President Brutus at Bristol University

After obtaining a Bachelor of Arts degree at Bristol, Brutus proceeded to Magdalen College of Oxford University to read another Bachelor's degree; this time in Politics, Philosophy and Economics. He completed this degree in 2 years and took another 2 years to study Modern Greats in a Master of Arts degree at Magdalen.

But why did our working-class hero choose to go to Oxford – a bastion of the English class system and home to the English aristocracy?

Brutus in Royal Company

By his own account, when it was first suggested to him that he might usefully study at Oxford, he flatly rejected the idea. The suggestion had come from Sir Phillip Morris as Vice Chancellor of Bristol University where he had completed his undergraduate studies. He had refuted the suggestion on the ground that: "Oxford, with its dreaming spires, was a bastion of English class attitudes; a home for aristocratic born-to-rulers and the embodiment of all the questionable elements of the English public school system.

"However, Sir Phillip insisted. His argument was that Oxford might well be all that I said it was but it was much more than that and I would have the excellent opportunity of taking exactly what I wanted from that learning experience.

"Sir Phillip, in all his wisdom, knew my anxieties about preserving and fostering my Caribbean identity. When he finally persuaded me, and I was accepted to read Modern Greats at Magdalen college, he told the President at Magdalen, Sir Thomas Boarse, 'This young man has some reservations about the cultural impact of Magdalen on him, but if I know anything about him, he is more likely to change Magdalen'.

"From that moment, I made some superficial gestures, like wearing red sweaters, simply to distinguish my 'Caribbean-ness' from the mournful subfix (dark suits and black gowns) which Oxford men wore. However empty the gesture was it underlined the fact that I was determined not to be unduly influenced by British class attitudes and values."

Brutus' education included not only academic pursuits but he also equipped himself well for the theatrical aspects of politics. He was also a fine actor with a special interest in poetic recitation. With Brutus' oratorical gifts and abilities, it was almost a public duty to be in politics.

In 1964, Brutus took up his first appointment as an Economist with the Commonwealth Secretariat in London where he only served for a brief period of 3 years.

In 1967, perhaps to the vigourous beckoning of destiny, Brutus "crossed the Rubicon" and returned to St. Lucia to set the stage for his fight with Caesar who had been in power for only 3 years.

But if Sir Phillip or Sir Thomas expected Brutus to betray his class upon returning to St. Lucia, they would have been sorely disappointed. As Brutus recalled: "On my return to St. Lucia, I felt I was unable to make any serious statement about my country until I had plunged back into the cultural wellsprings of life in St. Lucia. I had to unlearn Oxford and think and feel Caribbean."

Not for Brutus the spruce jacket-and-tie dress code that was the symbol of the status quo. For him it was military fatigues, cloth cap, and rubber boots that reached up to his knees as he launched himself into the phlegm of radical politics:

I wear army boots because I intend to mobilize this country always to walk tall. I wear a cap as the symbol of the worker. And I wear the colours of the revolution because the revolution is not quite over.

St. Lucia's Marcus Brutus: Speaking to a 1979 SLP Victory Rally

Brutus boasted several high degrees; but he was also a quixotic fantasist to a high degree. His speech at the victory rally typified the kind of doctrinaire Marxism that had come to characterize Brutus' rhetoric. Such public pronouncements stood as a monument to his enduring political infancy and immaturity; so tenuous, so romantic, his grip on reality.

Throughout his chequered political odyssey, Brutus inhabited a mythological, revolutionary universe; full of motifs of "armed struggle" and "revolution", with little of the substance appropriated in their time by such historical exponents.

Few in Caribbean politics presented a more caricature spectacle than our Brutus. All fire and bombast, it was a motif sprucely designed to appeal to the most facile, most gullible, most crude instincts of the youth who, at the height of his career, provided him with so much of their energy, and so much of their enthusiasm; but so little in the way of useful thinking.

Like in the run-up to the 1979 elections when he falsely and disingenuously promised the local dreadlocks community that he would "free up the herb" if the Labour Party had won the elections. During the above-quoted victory speech, if the credulous rasta brothers had come to hear the confirmation of Brutus' radical policy on narcotics, they would have been disappointed as what they heard from Brutus was not what they had bargained for. "Get off your backsides and work," was Brutus' dread exhortation to the dreads.

No matter; the disillusioned brethren would soon exact their revenge on the two-faced politician when he was snubbed and rebuffed by them during a riot in Castries in the aftermath of the 1979 elections. The would-be legalizer of marijuana's injunction to "get off the streets", and "protect your revolution" was ignored as the angry mobs almost reduced Castries to a plywood city.

Brutus' revolutionary zeal was not abated even by the victory of the SLP at the polls in 1979. As de facto leader of the new SLP Government, he vigorously pursued his dream of replacing the paramilitary police force with an army under his direct command "because the majority of the force remained loyal to the previous regime".

A strong supporter of the 1979 Grenada revolution, Brutus surreptitiously recruited a group of young St. Lucians to undergo military training in Cuba; unknown to the constitutional Prime Minister, Allan Louisy, who had, since the election victory, persistently accused unconstitutional Prime Minister Brutus of plotting to remove him by violent means.

And then there appeared an article in the *London Daily Telegraph* revealing that: "Not only had the new Labour Government of St. Lucia sent a group of one hundred men to Grenada for training by Cuban troops, the newly independent island's left-wing Government has recruited the young men for training as the nucleus of a people's revolutionary army...."

It is this spirit of refined imbecility that was the recurrent theme in the political failure of an otherwise great man; a simplicity and purity of mind demonstrating as it did that Brutus was not long on judgment; and certainly short on what, in a commonplace way, could be described as political commonsense; and, in a more mystical way, as political wisdom:

We have just seen Brutus, then, at his best and his worst; a virtuous man whose vices – not very serious vices, perhaps; vanity, inability to notice the vicious motives of those about him, a capacity to be deceived by analogies of his own making – undercut but do not vitiate the nobility of the character he demonstrates.

Norman Rabkin: Structure, Convention and Meaning in *Julius Caesar* (1958)

In reality, Brutus was not a radical and a communist any more than Errol Barrow, Forbes Burnham or Michael Manley.

But Errol Barrow, for example, was no Quixote – he was a realist. In an address to the Barbados Parliament on Land Rights, Conservatism and the Church on June 23, 1964, Barrow said: "… But what we are trying to do in Barbados is to give the people of this country an opportunity for education; a chance of getting a square meal; a chance of living in a decent house; a chance of getting a job for which they are qualified. These are the things we have been trying to do – and we have not created any revolution in this country."

Forbes Burnham was a crypto-communist sprucely dressed in the attire of the status quo in Guyana.

It took Michael Manley a two-term experimentation with socialism in Jamaica to come to terms with the sheer incongruity of doctrinaire socialism to the realities of small-island development:

It is idealists who create political terror; they are free from all desire for blood-shedding; but to them the lives of men and women are accidents; the lives of ideas are the true realities; and, armed with an abstract principle and a suspicion, they perform deeds which are at once beautiful and hideous.

Edward Dowden: Shakespeare – A Critical Study of His Mind and Art (1875)

Many times, Brutus would look over his life with regret. One day he lamented: "For a long time now, I have existed in St. Lucia as a kind of enigma. After a few years of close observation of the St. Lucian society following my return from study abroad, I came to the firm conclusion that no solid long-term development was possible until we had toughened the soft underbelly of the underprivileged and exploited sectors of the society. I discovered that St. Lucians were basically simple people conditioned by colonialism and religion to remain uncomplicated hewers of wood and drawers of water. Anyone who challenged the relationship between the hewers of wood and those who owned the means of production was immediately suspect."

In a world where politics is ruled by opinion polls that force politicians to be all things to all people Brutus remained steadfast to his beliefs; which probably explained why the people loved him but eschewed his rigid ideology. Such ambivalence often incurred the wrath of the "Big Brother", as he was affectionately called: "If you like me you must like my politics too," he would blare out in a deep, dark voice.

In his book entitled **It will be Alright in the Morning**, written in the aftermath of the historic 1974 elections, Rick Wayne wrote: "St. Lucians have never quite been able to decide whether to love [Brutus] as a husband might love a virtuous wife or with the slam-bang-see-you-later passion which is the house specialty of the professional harlot. It is as a quickie substitute to Premier [Julius Caesar] that [Brutus] is most loved by his people. They flock to him with their problems in much the same way that a cuckolded husband might run to a whore for canned comfort. [Brutus] is the quick relief balm of the bruised ego, the pain-relieving drug that must be discontinued as quickly as possible – to be used only when absolutely necessary, under strict medical supervision, for fear of possible adverse effects."

Among the many apparent contradictions in this ogre of a politician was the way he blended the granitic severity of his ideology with an almost paternalistic geniality when dealing with his flock. He was at once a populist and an intellectual. He could wear either a warm earthy smile or an expression of steel. He was simultaneously warm and stern. That was his originality; and that was his individuality. He nurtured something raw and simple in people, but did so as a philosopher and as a humanist.

Brutus among his flock

In his famous work, **The Pedagogy of the Oppressed** (1974), the Brazilian Educator, Paulo Freire, wrote: "A real humanist can be identified more by his trust in the people which engage him in their struggle, than by a thousand actions in their favour without that trust."

At Brutus' public appearances, people would come up to him and shake his hand, and sometimes kiss him (the latter act they probably would not relish with Julius Caesar). Brief encounters with Brutus suggested a nice man; longer acquaintances would confirm that. He radiated humour and decency. He was definitely more St. Lucian than Caesar in terms of geniality; never mind genealogy.

In the short-lived Labour Party Government, Brutus was deputy Prime Minister, Minister of Trade, Industry, Tourism and

Foreign Affairs. However, what evidence there is to show for Brutus' stewardship in Government is more anecdotal than substantial.

One of his more notable actions in Government was his arbitrary, unconstitutional and dictatorial closure of a local radio station whose management had disobeyed his orders. Such niggardliness on the part of Brutus raised more than a few eyebrows who had proclaimed "Peace, Freedom and Liberty!":

Live, Brutus! live! live!
Bring him with triumph home unto his house.
Give him a statue with his ancestors.
Let him be Caesar!

Shakespeare's *Julius Caesar*: Act III, Scene I

The role of the constitutional Prime Minister, Allan Louisy, in the "Quarrel Scene" is deserving of more space than can be accorded to it here. Suffice it to say that Allan Louisy turned out to be an altogether lousy Prime Minister. Even though he would publicly complain about persistent attempts by unconstitutional Prime Minister Brutus to overthrow him by violent means; he was, nevertheless, to boneless and too pusillanimous to fire him. He dared not touch Brutus.

Contrary to popular misconception, the "Quarrel Scene" between Brutus and Louisy did not have its genesis immediately following the 1979 SLP election victory over Caesar. It started in 1974 during the course of the SLP convention of that year in Augier when the Oxbridge heavyweight was humiliated in defeat by former puny High Court Judge Allan Louisy (a man he considered inferior to himself). Not even the consolation prize of second-in-command was enough to console the wounded intellectual. Moreover, that slight not only hit Brutus' ego for six but it also left him in a sulk that prevented him from ever accepting defeat:

The suggestion of vanity here increases immediately as Brutus mistakenly refuses to consider the possible aid that Cicero's oratory might give his cause. As Cassius, Casca and Cinna advance arguments, Brutus says nothing. Then Metellus, not knowing his man, uses terms predictably repellent to Brutus that Cicero may profitably be thought by the populace as the leader of the conspiracy:

METELLUS: *O let us have him for his silver hairs*
                   Will purchase us a good opinion,
                   And buy men's voices to commend our deeds.
                   It shall be said, his judgement ruled our hands;
                   Our youths and wildness shall no whit appear.
                   But all be buried in his gravity.

Whether touched under the circumstances by the crassness of Metellus' language or wounded by the thought that Cicero will get the credit for the leadership of the conspiracy, Brutus is wrong here; and his answer that Cicero will not deign to join another man's cabal, is trivial:

BRUTUS: *O name him not, let us not break with him,*
                 For he will never follow anything
                 That other men began.

Norman Rabkin: Structure, Convention, and Meaning in *Julius Caesar* (1958)

In the run-up to the 1979 elections, there was between Brutus and Louisy, a signed agreement, not to say a prenuptial agreement, whereby immediately following the political killing of Caesar in 1979, Louisy would hand over the leadership of the country to Brutus; his role as a Cicero-type figure in Shakespeare's *Julius Caesar* having been accomplished. Of course, that agreement was not worth the paper it was written on in that it was completely unconstitutional – a fact the Judge must have been only too aware of. Burtus, on the other hand, had apparently staked his entire political life on that agreement. It was when he challenged Louisy to "honour your agreement" that the "Quarrel Scene" began in earnest between the two men:

> *It is to be noted that "honour" is so strong in Brutus that Portia knows that she must play up to it; show herself as courageous, possessing a sense of "honour" like his. Brutus' obsession, almost to absurdity, with his thought is further evident from his long speech, prolixly expanding the idea that an oath is unnecessary to bind Romans to a noble enterprise:*

> BRUTUS: *No, not an oath. If not the face of men,*
> *The sufferance of our souls, the time's abuse.*
> *If there be motives weak, break off betimes.*
> *And every man hence to his idle bed*
> *So let high-sighted tyranny rage on*
> *Till each man drop by lottery.*

Wilson Knight: The Eroticism of *Julius Caesar* (1975)

By failing to fire Brutus following the defeat of Caesar in 1979, Louisy blundered both in tactics and in strategy. Tactically, he ignored to his bane the advice of Nicollo Machiavelli in **The**

Prince, who wrote: "Men must be either pampered or crushed because they can get revenge for small injuries but not for fatal ones. So any injury a prince does a man should be of such a kind that there is no fear of revenge."

Machiavelli would have seen Brutus' subsequent actions as not just predictable but certain.

Brutus, of course, was not without mountains of redeeming features. For example, corruption was one of the crusading issues that caused the political assassination of Caesar in 1979. Brutus had promised to restore morality to public life and clean up the administration of the country. However, the new SLP Government became even more corrupt than the previous regime; the SLP vision turning into a UWP revision.

Credit must be given to Brutus who was one of the few SLP Ministers and officials who steadfastly stood above the line of corruption and compromise. His honesty shone forth like diamonds scattered in the mire:

Caesar, upon whose death Brutus had agreed because of the corruption that power might bring, he comes to persuade himself had been "strucke ... but for supporting Robbers":

BRUTUS: *The name of Cassius honours this corruption*
          And chastisement doth therefore hide his head.

CASSIUS: *Chastisement!*

BRUTUS: *Did not great Julius bleed for justice's sake?*
          What villain touch'd his body, that did stab,
          And not for justice? What, shall one of us,
          That strucke the foremost man of all this world
          But for supporting Robbers, shall we now
          Contaminate our fingers with base bribes?

CASSIUS: *Do not presume too much upon my love;*
             I may do that I shall be sorry for.

BRUTUS: *You have done that you should be sorry for.*
             There is no terror, Cassius, in your threats;
             For I am arm'd so strong in honesty
             That they pass by me as the idle wind,
             Which I respect not.

**J.M. Stewart: Character and Motive in *Julius Caesar*
(1890)**

EPILOGUE I
ST. LUCIA'S MARCUS BRUTUS

Personally, I am very clear in my mind why a man of immense charm and suavity, and of whom I am rather fond, has failed totally in St. Lucia's politics. There are reasons. Firstly, he is grossly overrated and a consummate ass. His stint at Oxford University has obviously disadvantaged him. His repeated failures suggest that he was spewed out of Oxford and deposited in St. Lucia to be the perfect example of failure in politics. . . ."

Willie James: Columnist, Star Newspaper, July 18, 1987

It was a remarkable performance – a virtuoso exhibition of will power, and tenacity, which, after more than 30 years in the doldrums of political wilderness, kept him a public figure larger than anyone who held political power during the same period – save one. And up until his rather untimely death, he was still a feared and formidable politician with much to offer national as well as international politics. That he could still attract that level of public recognition said something, though perhaps merely of the sheer fascination exerted by the romantic figure in the wilderness and of tragic failure on a grand scale.

When one studies Brutus' long, rich, angry "struggles"; one begins to understand why, despite having been one of St. Lucia's finest sons of the 20th century, he was never able to wield political power.

Throughout his chequered political career, Brutus veritably acted like a man whom fate had dealt one of the grimmer parts in a Shakespearean tragedy:

Julius Caesar is a landmark not only in the history of Shakespearean tragedy but in the history of English tragedy. Before Brutus there had been no tragic hero whose character had combined noble grandeur with fatal imperfection. Heroes fatally imperfect there had been, as interest in tragic justice had grown and the old picture of a disorderly mortal ruled by fortune had faded, but many of them had been villains and weaklings and all of whom had been incapable of arousing profound admiration. In Brutus, then, Shakespeare discovered the noble hero with a tragic flaw.

Williard Farnhan: Shakespeare's Tragic Frontier: High-Minded Heroes (1950)

It is, at least, arguable that failure is far more edifying than success. Many writers, poets and artists, often no stranger to the condition themselves, have always lauded failure as a great improver of the human soul.

Listen to Hagel: "Pain has its rationale. It is a sign of life and a stimulus to reconstruction." On the matter of struggle, Hagel had this to say: "Struggle is the law of growth. Character is built in the storm and stress of the world and a man reaches his full height only through compulsions, responsibilities and suffering."

At the height of his failure in politics, Brutus had this to say about failure: "The failure syndrome is not a peculiarity of [Brutus]or St. Lucia alone. Any political observer can see the pattern throughout the islands. Tim Hector cannot emerge through the ballot box in Antigua nor Ralph Gonsalves in St.

Vincent. Rosie Douglas is an anomaly in Dominica and he might well be the exception which proved the rule. If he shows any persistent tendency to be serious about meaningful change in Dominica he will be dealt with through the oh-so democratic ballot box."

Months after the highly controversial (1974) elections... a well-wisher asked him why he continued to engage [Brutus] and Josie in what the friend suspected as a losing battle. [Caesar's] reply was: "St. Lucia is like a delicate little flower. A strong wind could blow it to kingdom come." Therefore it was imperative that [Caesar's] "little flower" be kept out of the hands of foolish virgins who are experts at spouting communist mumbo-jumbo and creating upheaval but could not be trusted to do anything constructive for the island's 130,000 population.

Rick Wayne: Star Newspaper Article entitled "St. Lucia's Man of the Century" (December 31, 1999)

To criticize without being prescriptive is to nag. Throughout his long odyssey in the political wilderness, Brutus became very adept at nagging. He could never be trusted to construct a bold, imaginative and transformational post-Caesar vision for St. Lucia – a fact that should never be underestimated when one probes Brutus' political failure.

By far, the most interesting item in respect of SLP Prime Minister Kenny Anthony's Budget of 2000-2001 was Brutus' contribution to that debate (which, as fate would have it, would be his last in the House of Assembly). In a manner reminiscent to his contribution to the 1980/81 Budget debate when he brought down the Louisy Government, Brutus went almost beyond the call of duty to admonish a stunned Prime Minister Anthony that his fortunes were waning and that there was a hardening of feeling on the ground against the 3-year old Government.

"I rise to debate this Budget with the rising tide of my personal history threatening to choke me or silence me. My history, Mr. Speaker, is a history of struggle, not necessarily a struggle to reduce principalities and Kings but a struggle to empower the ordinary people who I have dedicated my life to serve.

"My relationship with the people I serve has given me some measure of authority but it has also burdened me with a heavy responsibility between the collective responsibility to my Cabinet colleagues and the spiritual nexus I have with the people who created me and sustained me.

"Mr. Speaker, I heard the excellent throne speech by Dame Pearlette Louisy. That speech tried to give the psychological framework for the Budget. It struck some very interesting, exciting and fundamental chords when she spoke of the elemental humanity that binds us irrespective of race, religion or politics. There was a feeling that she was grappling with fundamentals – a future which this Government faces.

"There is a serious attempt in Government to grapple with fundamentals but sometimes there is very little praise for long-term projections. We have seen a lot of evidence of that in the Budget presented by the Minister of Finance who saw attempts to review the constitution as fundamental as well as, say attempts to review the criminal code or the civil law.

"Mr. Speaker, there is a serious dichotomy in the country between the Government's claim that it is working and performing more than any other previous Government had done and the mass disillusionment with the Government for its non-performance and its schizophrenic profile in saying one thing and doing another. Whether there is validity in this general perception, each one of us must decide. What is the Government we must come to terms with?

"It is the public perception that it is so. To challenge this label our Government should be assiduous in its transparency. We must avoid the clever devilry of giving a concession with one hand and taking it back with another. We must not use flashing mirrors to blind the eyes of the people; they must be convinced that the Government is honest and straightforward with its citizens and then the people will be prepared to march to hell and back behind them.

"The Senate is a Chamber of review and this in itself predisposes a capacity to criticize and a capacity to adjudicate. Against this background the decision to fire a Senator who voted against a Bill is curious to say the least. But the decision to dismiss Senators who abstained seems a direct affront to the democratic process. This action weakens democracy and certainly does not strengthen it. Conversely, such action sends a distressing message about free speech and expression. It strengthens autocracy and highly centralized decision-making.

"Mr. Speaker, I could not forget the reading lines of John Milton in his clarion call for the freedom to speak: 'Give me the courage to speak, to argue, to utter freely according to my conscience above all other liberties.'

"Mr. Speaker, I have tried in the course of this address to extrapolate from her Excellency's throne speech the positives which should give directions, purpose and guidance to the Government and its programmes. I have identified areas in which actions of the Government veered away from the principles of the throne speech. I have warned repeatedly about this kind of ambivalence and suggested that this might be one of the many factors which have eroded popular trust in the Government.

"I can see that the disenchantment is not island-wide. There are places in the rural areas where people are pleased and grateful for the basic amenities which this Government has brought to them. On the other hand the urban areas and their suburbs are more solidly in the embrace of the media and a strong antipathy towards the Government is certainly taking hold in most communities.

"We must note that the public gallery in this House is almost as empty in the course of this Budget debate as it was when the previous Government was plumbing the depths of its unpopularity.

I have tried to explain and analyze this phenomenon. It is not easy; it is new. It took the United Workers' Party 30 years to follow this graph of decline and it is almost inexplicable that this Government should race headlong down this road in three measly years – after the brilliant record of performance we heard from every speaker in this debate.

"In the course of the Prime Minister's Budget address, it was obvious that fundamental issues were being tackled; such as the review of the constitution, the review of the criminal and civil codes, a legislative programme that is almost mind-boggling. Amidst all this there have been many instances of inexperience and bungling. But this is inevitable since the electorate chose to return a young and inexperienced cadre of representatives to run the country. It was a paradigm shift from the over-the-hill image of the previous Government.

"As Budgets go, this is a classical Budget. It does all the things that pre-election budgets do. It purports not to tax the electorate; it balances beautifully as modern economies try to do; it gives out the pork-barrel demands of the communities; it caters for the contribution of savings to the investment programme; it spreads sugar where the cake is burnt as in the duty concessions to the taxi-men. In fact, it is a clever Budget but somehow, it fails to address the central dilemma of the Government.

"Why should a show of brilliant governance result in the alienation of all the important sectors of the community? Why have we alienated the media? Why have we as a Government alienated the private sector? Why have we alienated the farmers? Why have we alienated the public servants? Why have we alienated the teachers? Why have we alienated the churches? Why have we alienated some trusted stalwarts? Why have we alienated the Opposition? Even them we can embrace. We probably have alienated some of our regional colleagues.

"Mr. Speaker, this situation calls for some serious in-depth introspection. More than public relations people must insist that an ounce of image is worth a pound of performance. I am not about to suggest that this Government should concentrate on image at the expense of performance, especially as the Government is already well-endowed with spin doctors.

"Perhaps the solution might be to keep the collective ear of the Government nearer the ground. I am, Mr. Speaker, the most travelled member of the Government. My frequent absences from this Honourable House attests to this but whenever I am in the State I travel along the length and breadth of St. Lucia to ensure that I am in touch with what the ordinary man in the street is saying. This is the touchstone of my politics. So I am able to give my colleagues advice and guidance as to what people are saying on the ground. Sometimes, we must be humble enough to bow to the voice of the people who have put us in these elevated positions.

"Mr. Speaker, I have no illusions about my locus standi in Government. The appointment of two deputy Prime Ministers indicated clearly that I was removed from the red meat of decision-making. I have no quarrel with that and I have worked in tandem with them and with all my colleagues. I do not harbour rancour in politics and I have absolutely no ambitions. My only ambition is to see a sound people-oriented Government for St. Lucia in the new Millennium."

Brutus was shortly thereafter fired by Prime Minister Kenny Anthony for what he saw as Brutus' ingratitude:

> ANTHONY: *This was the most unkindest cut of all,*
> *For when the noble Caesar saw him stab,*
> *Ingratitude, more strong than traitor's arms,*
> *Quite vanquished him: then burst his mighty heart;*
> *And, in his mantle muffling up his face,*
> *Even at the base of Pompey's statua,*
> *Which all the while ran blood, great Caesar fell.*
> *O! what a fall was there, my countrymen.*

Shakespeare's *Julius Caesar*: Act III, Scene II

And then, in 2003, the last year of his mortal life, the following volley of articles started appearing in Brutus' CRUSADER Newspaper critical of Prime Minister ANTHONY, the Editorial Writer being Brutus himself:

"THE THIRTY MILLION DOLLAR DECEPTION!

"We must offer a tongue-in-cheek thanks to Mr. Anthony Atkinson, the Liquidator for Pigeon Point Hotel Ltd., for the convenient bit of information which he volunteered. Fairmont hotel did not put in a bid for the Hyatt Hotel.

"This disclosure was manna from heaven for the hired guns to venture out in defence of the Government. We all know that this is technically true but it is certainly not the whole story. Fairmont Hotel was active in trying to purchase the bonds directly from Royal Merchant Bank all during the time the bidding process was on. But these details are of little interest to the general public and Mr. Atkinson has no obligation to inform the public.

"The obligation rests solely on the shoulders of the Prime Minister to lift the veil of secrecy and deception from the transaction surrounding the purchase of the Hyatt Hotel. The Prime Minister is the custodian of the public monies and he is personally accountable to the people of St. Lucia for the way these monies are spent. We should not be scratching around for information on such a transaction and neither Mr. Atkinson nor spin doctor Bousquet can offer placebos to vitiate the public RIGHT TO KNOW.

"Every detail of this transaction should have been before the public if thirty million dollars of public funds is involved and of course only St. Lucian taxpayers would have to foot the bill. The most startling revelation from Mr. Atkinson was the admission that he knew nothing about the Government's thirty million dollar stake in the Hyatt Hotel until he read about it in the local press! This is both alarming and amazing!

"But there is a reason for this. The Prime Minister went out of his way to conceal the details of Government's involvement in providing massive loans for cost overruns, not only from the public but even from the House of Assembly. When he finally got around to slipping the Resolution through the House of Assembly eight days before Christmas, the information given to the legislators was nothing short of scandalous. Absolutely no documentation was presented to the House except a sketchy Resolution which contradicted itself on the purpose for which a loan of US$41 million was being sought.

"The Prime Minister has an incisive mind and he is legally trained but the apology for an explanation which he treated his colleagues to was an insult to the intelligence of the entire nation. When the Prime Minister becomes befuddled, vague, inaccurate and cloudy, it is by DESIGN and not by chance. It was a clear attempt to keep both the House and the public in the dark about this deal.

"The Hansard (Record of Parliamentary Debates) of 17th December 2002, pages 19 to 25, should be read by all interested persons as a study in obfuscation and deception. Nothing is crystal clear, everything is vague and confused and sometimes bordering on GOBBLEDEGOOK.

"Here is an excerpt from page 22 of the Hansard: '... If we needed an additional hotel we needed to go an extra mile. The question was how could that be done? In the circumstances after the Government reviewed all the options, the Government agreed to a formula to the following effect, that the Bank will proceed to give the hotel support up to a prescribed amount, 11 million dollars (US) to take care of possible cost overruns. That agreement was titled a Put Option Agreement, meaning in effect that it does not crystallise into a guarantee or a loan immediately. It will only crystallise if at the end of the day the hotel fails and at that point it becomes an obligation for which the Government will then go through the usual processes. In essence that is what it was.'

"What a masterpiece in trickery, flashing mirrors and skullduggery! That statement poses more questions that it answers. Should the public not know what were the other options open to the Government? Which Bank was he referring to? To whom would the loan funds go? To Rochamel, to Pigeon Point Hotel Ltd., or to the nebulous Hyatt? How did the Prime Minister arrive at the ceiling figure of US$11 million for POSSIBLE cost overruns? Not actual cost overruns but POSSIBLE cost overruns?

"What is a PUT OPTION agreement? Another flashing mirror? How can a guarantee to lend thirty million dollars not be a guarantee until the borrower fails to repay? Is this a device to circumvent the law of the land? What about the Administration of Finance Act which requires parliamentary approval BEFORE any guarantee is made by Government?

"What is meant by our OBLIGATION to Hyatt? What is the real nature of this so-called OBLIGATION. How can a loan not be a loan until it CRYSTALLISED into a loan? What clever devilry is our Prime Minister using to mesmerize the House of Assembly and the people of St. Lucia?

"Let us look again at another excerpt from the Prime Minister's address in the same Hansard: '… that the Government agreed to give further support until such time as the option can materialize, because the option was that it may not have materialized at all or that it would materialize and it did materialize given the events of September 11th and the closure of the Hotel.'

"Why this almost unintelligible DOUBLE-TALK? Is the Prime Minister trying to inform or enlighten the House and the people, or is he bent on confusing us? This confusing diction drips with deception. Get on with it and tell our people clearly why you are endangering thirty million dollars of their money! Who exactly are you lending it to? Why do you find it necessary to take this inordinate risk? What will the people get from it? What steps have you taken to protect this mammoth investment in a private venture?

"You are slipping this surreptitiously through the House of Assembly many months AFTER the liquidation of Hyatt and not even the Liquidator Mr. Atkinson is aware that the Government has a thirty million dollar claim on the assets of the liquidated company! Is the Prime Minister not the official Protector of the Public Purse? Why did he not move heaven and earth to ensure that a claim was registered to recover the people's money? Was he waiting for the loan to CRYSTALLISE into a loan?

"Oh what a tangled web we weave, when first we practice to deceive!

"One of the structural weaknesses of the Anthony Administration is a kind of intellectual arrogance bolstered by a strong majority in the Assembly. The combination of these two factors creates an illusion of omnipotence. They can pull any kind of stunt and the assumption is that the general public is too docile, to UNINFORMED and too indifferent to take notice. It is this illusion of infallibility and omnipotence which has landed the Minister of Finance in this horrible mess.

"One of the main devices for protecting sleazy transactions is to deny or withhold information regarding the transaction. The public is then left free to speculate or attribute motives if the necessary information is not forthcoming.

"The Prime Minister's address to the House as reported in Hansard was a study in evasiveness and deception. He simply could not reveal the real story of this incredible saga. He had already jumped out of his crease on Rick Wayne's Talk Show to set up the green lights for sandal's acquisition of the Hotel. In doing so he turned on its head the entire Party Policy regarding All-inclusive Hotels and made it clear to the St. Lucian public that his Government had no objection to Sandals acquiring and owning the Hotel.

"When Fairmont appeared on the scene using an entity called Cypress Asset Management LP to purchase the bonds directly from the Bank and offering to take care of all the creditors, the shutters went up and even the Bank imposed a stringent condition by requesting that the company wishing to purchase the bonds for the Hotel should make a payment of a non-refundable deposit of US$19 million as a pre-condition for purchase.

"Fairmont (or shall we say Cypress) justifiably felt that the cards were being stacked against them and this resulted in a Court case between Pigeon Point Hotel Ltd., and the Royal Merchant Bank. In the end Fairmont did not submit a bid and the interested persons were fully aware that Fairmont was being sandbagged.

"A full public relations campaign was launched in St. Lucia to promote the Sandals' bid. WHY? Was it in the public interest or was there a sinister conspiracy for less public reasons? Would the Sandals acquisition protect our thirty million dollar stake or was that a forgotten throw-away? At least the Fairmont initiative offered to cover all creditors but because of our Prime Minister's double-talk we are not clear whether the thirty million was a loan or an un-crystallised gift!

"The Labour Party has always been very keen on claiming FIRSTS. They can confidently claim this one – that no Leader in St. Lucia's political history ever attempted a sleight-of-hand so outrageous, so massive, so cynical, so bastardly, so illegal and so contemptuous of the people.

"This one reckless throw of the dice involving so much of our scarce public funds has cast a very dark shadow on the financial integrity of the Government. It also begs a serious question as to whether the Anthony Government and New Labour ever had the interest of the people at heart or whether they used the slogan and rhetoric of Labour to seize power and reverted to type when the scepter was in their grip."

May 17, 2003

"THE $30 MILLION FIASCO: THOSE EXTRAORDINARY STEPS

"Thus did Prime Minister and Minister of Finance, Dr. Kenny Anthony, describe the Rochamel affair in his interview on Radio St. Lucia on Monday evening: 'Some extraordinary steps are necessary to be taken at times in the business of Government.'

"When those 'extraordinary steps' are taken, not in the interest of, and unknown to the people, then there is a grave breach in the 'Contract of Faith'.

"For several months after that controversy had surfaced, the Prime Minister and Minister of Finance had been steadfastly and perseveringly reluctant to give any explanation of his action to the people of St. Lucia; declaring at one stage that that was a 'private matter'.

"Then, in the face of mounting island-wide criticism for his silence, instead of making his 'explanation' at a Press Conference, or at a sitting of the House of Assembly, he chose to conceal himself from the eyes of a skeptical public and have a relatively inexperienced party supporter at Radio St. Lucia interview him. The questions were not only nonsensical, but innocuously framed, and the Prime Minister's performance in all this was singularly and pathetically unimpressive. He resolutely avoided giving any specific answers.

"The burning question, which has yet to be answered, is: Was Parliamentary approval, as required by law, sought by the Minister of Finance, for that guarantee to Rochamel for those 'cost overruns'? If not, then the Minister of Finance had acted illegally. What were the terms of the Agreement made by the Minister of Finance in December 1997? Will he make that public? The public has a right to know.

"All that the people demand is that the Prime Minister and Minister of Finance explain his action to the satisfaction of the people; but he has skirted the issues and continues to do so, creating, instead, a smokescreen to cloud the issues and, hopefully, divert the people's attention. Hence the speculation which is rife throughout the island and that, we might add, is an unhealthy state of affairs.

"Dr. Anthony is always quick to threaten his critics, and those threats are not often veiled either. On Monday evening, he was at his old game again, saying that any suggestion of corruption by him or his Government would not be tolerated or taken lightly. Dr. Anthony thus regards himself as being above criticism. He is the infallible one.

"No one is accusing Dr. Anthony of corruption. Was he not the one who had accused the former administration of widespread corruption? And went further, deeming it absolutely necessary to have an inquiry into those alleged acts of corruption, an inquiry which cost the country millions of dollars?

BRUTUS: *The name of Cassius honours this corruption*
And chastisement doth therefore hide his head.

CASSIUS: *Chastisement!*

BRUTUS: *Did not great Julius bleed for justice's sake?*
What villain touch'd his body, that did stab,
And not for justice? What, shall one of us,
That strucke the foremost man of all this world
But for supporting Robbers, shall we now
Contaminate our fingers with base bribes?

CASSIUS: *Do not presume too much upon my love;*
I may do that I shall be sorry for.

BRUTUS: *You have done that you should be sorry for.*
There is no terror, Cassius, in your threats;
For I am arm'd so strong in honesty
That they pass by me as the idle wind,
Which I respect not.

Shakespeare's *Julius Caesar*: Act IV, Scene II

"And the two former Prime Ministers whom he had deliberately targeted, out of the purest of mischief, did not the English lawyer who had conducted the inquiry exonerate those two Prime Ministers; and even called specifically for Dr. Anthony to apologize to one in particular, Dr. Vaughan Lewis? Did Dr. Anthony do so? Of course not! He considers himself too high and mighty for that: 'He doth bestride the world like a colossus and we petty men must peep about and find ourselves dishonourable graves.'

"St. Lucia is not an isolated spot of land in some remote part of the universe, nor is it in some other distant galaxy, Dr. Anthony. If, perhaps, your knowledge of geography is as scanty as your knowledge and understanding of Economics and Finance, St. Lucia is very much part of this planet. So its political problems are common knowledge and the subject of much discussion throughout the world, and you feature as the chief protagonist.

"This arrogant, insolent, insulting and obfuscatory behaviour on the part of the Prime Minister in his treatment of the people of St. Lucia, as though he has no legal obligation or moral responsibility to be accountable for his actions, is unbecoming of an elected Member of Parliament. He and his colleagues were elected by the people of St. Lucia and had come to high office, not by any divine right to which they and they alone are entitled.

"The St. Lucia Labour Party had presented itself to the electorate in 1997 as a body of people united for promoting the national interest and upon their declared promise of transparency in Government. This Government has grown exorbitant in the use of its powers, because of the absolute majority in the House.

"The people are aggrieved and have the right to dismiss this Government for its breach of promise and for breaking the trust that the people had placed in them."

May 24, 2003

"NO APOLOGY, SAYS DR. ANTHONY

"A Hopelessly lackluster Market Steps Meeting on Thursday night disappointed even supporters of the St. Lucia Labour Party who hoped to hear Prime Minister Anthony's explanation for the cost overrun guarantee given to Rochamel for the construction of the Hyatt Hotel. The meeting failed to attract the level of attendance which the ruling Party expected.

"There was no warmth and bounce back from the crowd despite the laboured efforts from the speakers to drum up a flicker of support and encouragement from the listeners.

"It was very much an outing for the Second Eleven as Chairman Damian Greaves announced that Ministers Mario Michel, Calixte George and Felix Finisterre were all out of the State on official business. The early speakers included Ignatius Jean and Petrus Compton with Phillip Pierre and Prime Minister Anthony winding up.

"The strategy was clearly to leave the Rochamel issue to the Prime Minister but his treatment of the issue was still evasive. He attempted a historical account of the whole transaction; adding very little in new information to the accounts which were bandied around in the Media for the past few weeks.

"Most St. Lucians were anxious to hear the Prime Minister's explanation to the charge that he had given a cost overrun guarantee to Rochamel without seeking the prior approval of the House of Assembly as required by the Administration of Finance Act of 1997. Somewhat weakly, the Prime Minister repeated the argument which he used in the House of Assembly that the guarantee was not a guarantee until the Government was required to refund the bank for funds disbursed to Rochamel. He referred to this as a PUT OPTION.

"In the past few weeks the media has rejected this explanation as frivolous and laughable and questioned the device as an attempt to circumvent the law of the land. In his House of Assembly remarks, the Prime Minister stated categorically that he had agreed to authorize the Bank to disburse funds not exceeding US$11 million to the construction company by way of a guarantee of cost overruns.

"The double-talk continued on the Market Steps with the Prime Minister fighting desperately to portray himself as a man of integrity who is always operating in the interest of the workers. He cited the Step Programme and the Belle Fashions bail-out as evidence of his pro-worker stance and tried hard to convince the crowd that his thirty million dollar gift to Rochamel was to provide jobs for St. Lucian workers.

"The level of disbelief and cynicism in the community surrounding this sleazy transaction is so high that Prime Minister Anthony was forced to dance around in wild attacks on the Media and a variety of Media personalities. He focused heavily on Newsmaker Live's Timothy Poleon for describing his actions as 'subterfuge' and attacked [me] as the Great Satan who will soon have to RENOUNCE THE DEVIL!

"He exempted TV Host Rick Wayne from his diatribe against the Media, claiming that Rick Wayne said that he did not believe that the Prime Minister would be part of any corruption and that Rick Wayne had apologized for printing an article from Sir John Compton referring to Ministers as a 'band of looters'.

"When speakers tried desperately to portray themselves as models of integrity, somehow it gave away the game; it is precisely because their dubious action and dealings give rise to widespread suspicion and cynicism.

"It was an uphill battle for Prime Minister Anthony tying to cut through the cool aloofness of an audience which was simply seeking for explanatory information which would dispel the doubts and suspicion. No direct charges of dishonesty had been levelled at the Prime Minister and his Government but the failure to provide the necessary documentation and data has resulted in mounting suspicion and anger."

May 31, 2003

"THE OATH OF ALLEGIANCE:
BOLTING THE STABLE DOOR

"There is a character in local folklore known as ALEXIE GRANDE MOVEMENT! Alexie is a showy and expressive extrovert who indulges in exaggerated gestures and overdone theatrical poses. But Alexie was also a spinner of yarns and imaginary stories. He is in addition A PATHOLOGICAL LIAR and when Alexie is in his most expansive style – waving his hands in grand empty gestures, that's when he unleashes his most vicious lie! Prime Minister Anthony fits snugly into this folkloric character.

"Those of us who know the Prime Minister's body language well can easily tell when he is about to drop a whopper! Despite all his red hearings about persons taking Cabinet business and documents to the public, it was the same body language which undid him in the Rochamel affair. He tried to deceive the House of Assembly by waving what purported to be a copy of the Hansard Report and invited everyone to read it in order to find a full explanation of the Rochamel Affair.

"Well, all the tell-tale signals of bluff and duplicity were there so I hurried the very next day to purchase a copy of the Hansard from the Clerk of the Parliament for $25.00. This was easily the best $25.00 ever spent! With absolutely no other information or documents whatever, I studied the Hansard and discovered that we had stumbled upon one of the most outrageous acts of deception in the history of St. Lucian politics, if not in the annals of Caribbean politics.

"The decision to authorize the guarantee of a massive sum of money for the cost overruns of a private construction company engaged in building the Hyatt Hotel in St. Lucia was fraught with difficulties; the main one being that the Prime Minister had not the legal authority to commit this kind of money to a venture of this kind.

"The law is clear and unambiguous on this point and even laymen can understand it far less one with the avowed, self-confessed brilliance of Dr. Anthony in such legalistic matters. Was this his legal blind spot? Or is it a question of there being none so blind as those who would not see!

"One of the more obvious character traits of the Prime Minister is to distract attention from vital issues by attributing blame to others. Curiously enough, in this Rochamel affair, he has targeted me as being responsible, since I was a member of Cabinet when the decision was taken to pay cost overruns to Rochamel. In addition, he accuses me of being responsible for divulging the details of this Cabinet transaction to the public. He is also insinuating that I was in possession of relevant Cabinet documents and agreements.

"I can remember clearly being present at a Cabinet meeting when Rochamel representatives attended in order to present their proposals and request concessions from Cabinet. At that time, the question of cost overruns was not foremost in their discussion, although it was mentioned. The interest of Cabinet seemed more focused on preserving areas of the Hotel site for public use and a committee was formed with this foremost in mind.

"I was not particularly averse to granting some assistance on cost overruns, but never in my wildest dreams did I envisage such astronomical figures with which we are now confronted. I am not in possession of any documents relating to Rochamel neither do I possess any Cabinet papers which will throw light on the Rochamel Project. I must hasten to add that in the event that I possessed such documents I would have no hesitation in sharing the details with the general public.

"One of the greatest sins of omission in this whole Rochamel escapade is the failure of the Prime Minister and his Government to show some measure of transparency and accountability to the people that they purport to represent. It has been a cardinal principle of my political involvement to be as open and transparent as possible with the general public and when mammoth sums of their money is involved, financial probity demands such exposure and accountability.

"It seems to be characteristic of the New Labour Regime to bolt the stable door after the horse has escaped. The gesture of holding Cabinet secretary press briefings, smacks of being too little too late. Once again the mirrors are flashing. Parallel with those gestures of openness the Prime Minister is seeking to impose higher conditions of secrecy in the conduct of Government business. He gives with one hand and takes back with the other!

"The most casual observer of St. Lucian politics will concede that there is a massive breach of trust between the Government of Prime Minister Anthony and the people of St. Lucia on the Rochamel issue. Most people are convinced that the Prime Minister did not act in the public interest in conducting this transaction.

"As a matter of fact he displayed a serious dereliction of duty in not protecting the patrimony of the people from scandalous adventurers. This last Rochamel episode convinced the St. Lucian public of what they had suspected a long time that Dr. Anthony was not operating in the interest of the people.

"It was this realization which spanned this new idea of a new Oath of Allegiance. From my very first encounter with the Oath of Allegiance when I was sworn in as a Minister of Government in 1979, I instinctively bristled at the fact that we owe allegiance only to the Queen of England at the expense of the people of St. Lucia.

"It was not so much an anti-monarchical statement, it was a genuine attempt to place the people at the center of our political ethos. At the swearing ceremony, I amended the text to reflect this and observed the discomfort and chagrin of the then speaker of the House, Hon. Wilfred St. Clair Daniel. Seventeen years later, when Dr. Anthony formed his Government he never felt disposed to amend this code.

"His has been six years in office and was not tempted to make any such amendment until it became clear to him that he needed a gimmick to repair the sizable rift between the Government and the people who elected him. **The motive for this amendment of the Oath of Allegiance is clearly opportunistic and not based on the principle of the elevation of the people of St. Lucia.** (Author's emphasis)

"Had Dr. Anthony been seriously and genuinely interested in demonstrating his new-found respect for the people of St. Lucia, he would start with a candid and open disclosure of all the details and documents surrounding the Rochamel transaction.

"Even at this mysterious late stage he has thrown up another conflicting figure to the House of Assembly which he claims is the *real* amount of cost overruns. In this steamy atmosphere of deceit and duplicity how can we rely on the word of a Finance Minister, and a legally trained one at that, who willfully flouts the most basic legal requirements for committing the money of the people entrusted to the Consolidated Fund?

"The people should not be fooled by the flashing mirrors of Dr. Anthony and his New Labour cohorts!"

July 12, 2003

"MARTINUS TRIUMPHS! JUDGE GRANTS FULL DICLOSURE

"The entire nation has been united in its call for FULL DISCLOSURE in the Rochamel AFFAIR. The media has been consistently strident in requesting that our Prime Minister should make a clean breast of everything and put all documents and agreements at the disposal of the general public. The Ministers of Government have all maintained a stony silence, presumably to protect their salaries despite the common knowledge that some of them are critical of the Prime Minister's role in the Rochamel Affair.

"The Prime Minister himself has shown incredible arrogance in fending off questions and enquires. He has made attempts to accommodate the media in response to a highly charged public demand. But these responses raise more questions than they satisfied. His posture in venturing to placate the media was not only arrogant but defensive, in that he provided a number of statistics which gave the clear impression that he was bent on concealing the truth. This was a tremendous volte-face for a regime that had prided itself on transparency and full accountability.

"In this week's hearing before Justice Shanks, the scenario was weird to say the least. The well-paid and frequently used Senior Counsel from Dominica made no appearance on the first day and left the encounter in the hands of a Junior Counsel, Ms. Veronica Cenac. The sparring which followed between **Mr. Martinus François** who championed the cause and Ms Cenac representing the Prime Minister was unfortunate. It projected the defence as being totally against the full disclosure of information and more concerned with extracting an adjournment.

"The ruling of the Judge that there should be full disclosure of all the relevant documents was a triumph for Barrister **Martinus François** who stuck himself out on this vital issue when his legal colleagues remained timid and pusillanimous. It all seemed so totally unnecessary that all the paraphernalia of a judicial hearing had to be pursued in order to extract from our Prime Representative information which properly belongs to the People themselves. The crowning irony is that the astronomical fees, which will be paid to the Senior Counsel, will no doubt come from the public purse and not from the pocket of Dr. Anthony.

"After the matter surfaced in Court on Thursday, Senior Counsel Astaphan promptly contacted the local media and embarked on a spirited defence of Dr. Anthony. His action seemed to set new standards for forensic practice in the Caribbean. Mr. Astaphan invaded the media in the tradition of a Spin Doctor rather than a traditional Defence Counsel. He was bent on portraying an image of the Prime Minister as a champion of public disclosure when the opposite was so painfully obvious to St. Lucians who were more familiar with the Rochamel saga than Mr. Astaphan.

"He pleaded earnestly that his client, Dr. Anthony, had instructed him to grant the full disclosure of all documents to the Courts and allow the hearing to take its full course with no attempt to short-circuit the due process of the law. Three cheers for Mr. Astaphan in his public relations effort to make his Prime Ministerial Client look good to prospective voters.

"Perhaps this is a whole new set of legal ethics which Mr. Astaphan is pursuing but in his anxiety to white wash his client, he was prepared to demean and discredit the Junior Counsel who stood in for him at the hearing. He laid all the blame at her door claiming that he had given full instructions to the Attorney General's office regarding public disclosure of documents.

"He went on to suggest that there might have been a communications problem with his Junior Counsel and it might be necessary to replace her with Senior Counsel to hold briefs during his absence. Was all this necessary over the public media? Or was his desperation in trying to project a certain image of his client so acute?

"It was certainly not in the finest tradition of the legal profession for Mr. Astaphan to resort to such cheap shots in projecting a creditable political image for his client. Perhaps the scale of fees in these quasi-political cases provides the incentive for Counsel to overstep the niceties of legal representation and venture into the vulgarity of political promotion.

"But whatever spin Mr. Astaphan wishes to put on last Thursday's proceedings, the bottom line is that the Courts have called for FULL DISCLOSURE of documents. Already many Rochamel observers are licking their lips to discover the document which authorized the Bank to disburse funds as a result of a Government Guarantee to provide eleven million US dollars to the Construction Company. This document which appeared to have satisfied the RBTT Bankers could not possibly have had the legal seal of Resolution from the House of Assembly. It is this type of concern which Mr. Astaphan must apply his legal skills to, instead of vilifying Junior Counsel for the greater glory of his client.

"If it is found that Prime Minister Anthony had committed a gross breach of the laws of this country in not getting the prior approval of the House of Assembly, the question arises as to what should be done. Talk Show Host Rick Wayne points out regularly that there are no sanctions in the Administration of Finance Act for Ministers of Finance who trash the laws of the state in this way.

"In America the President would be impeached. In England the conventions would require immediate resignation or dismissal of the offending Minister. But in St. Lucia, where conventions are not respected and corrupt beneficiaries are prepared to stick like barnacles to the ship of State, it will require all the muscle and creativity of the People of St. Lucia to punish offending Ministers.

"Rick Wayne has stressed repeatedly that he is averse to any moves for change which would create chaos in our society at this point in time. He has been tireless in spurring St. Lucians on to action in taking the issues of governance into their own hands but invariably he stops short with his little caveat about chaos. But he, more than anyone else, is aware that political eggs must be broken to make social omelettes of change and reform.

"**Mr. Martinus François'** day in Court is of extreme importance to the cause of Justice in St. Lucia today. We are under the aegis of a reckless and acquisitive Regime and the prevailing mood of the people is raw and vengeful. The Rochamel Affair is a dangerous symbol of the recklessness of Prime Minister Anthony and it will require all the creativity and resourcefulness of the Community to dispense justice and punishment without 'rising the stones of Rome to mutiny'."

July 19, 2003

"IS ROCHAMEL THE PROMISED ARMAGEDDON?

"One of the most heart-wrenching and difficult decisions I have taken in my political career was the decision to quit the post of Ambassador to the United Nations and return to contest elections and shape a new political path for St. Lucia and OECS politics. The decision was critical because I had attained a fairly high level of acceptability in the United Nations and was poised to reap tremendous benefits for St. Lucia. My stint as Deputy President of the General Assembly and the ratings I received for on-the-floor speeches at the Assembly stimulated a profile which put me in touch with all the main developed and developing countries that comprise the United Nations.

"This personal relationship had the possibility of generating tremendous benefits for our small-island State. I had already forged a close attachment with the Government of China as the foremost developing country. But the prime consideration which clogged this diplomatic thrust into development was my realization that the images and perception coming out of the political arena in St. Lucia were largely negative. There were weekly strikes in the banana industry and a general political unrest which created a bleak impact on possible investors and people wishing to do business with our country.

"I had the clear impression that superficial changes would not redound to the economic interest of the island unless and until we had settled our political problems in a radical and reassuring way. The game of musical cheers played by Compton and Lewis was certainly not a credible move in stabilizing the country. It was my view that the Compton regime should be removed and a strong, competent and progressive Government should take St. Lucia into the new century. Despite the cynical urgings of Kenny Anthony this decision had nothing to do with bouts of prime-ministeritis. It originated in a deep passion for the orderly growth and development of a country and people that I loved so much.

"The outcome of this bold step into the reconstruction of our country ran into a number of snags culminating in the disastrous collapse of the Alliance for National Unity in 2001. Needless to say, we had succeeded in establishing what looked like a solid Government in 1997 under the leadership of Dr. Kenny Anthony with a parliamentary majority which was historic. It would be invidious at this point for me to trace the graph of decline which has reduced the regime to such a parlous state today. But I am clear in my conscience that I had chronicled both in public and in private the pitfalls which confronted the Government at every step along the way.

"Quite clearly the Anthony Regime had its own agenda and was bent on elevating cliques at the expense of the ordinary man. More than that they exploited the ignorance of the ordinary man by fooling him and confusing him with public relations gimmicks. They were careful to establish an elaborate public relations machinery complete with highly paid spin doctors to provide placebos for the public while they promote their own agenda.

"We listened to reckless flights of fancy about Armageddon on public platforms. The St. Lucian public was totally confused by this weird reference to this biblical battle. What could possibly be the connection between the politics of St. Lucia and a cataclysmic event like Armageddon? Were we on the verge of the mother of all political battles? Were St. Lucians faced with total economic ruin? Or were we about to encounter a massive political hoax which would redefine the entire political history and development of St. Lucia for many generations to come?

"Many political analysts see the Rochamel Affair as having all the dreaded dimensions of an Armageddon. Judging from the Judicial Order handed down by Justice Shanks in the Rochamel Case it is clear that the distinguished Judge perceives the submission before him as a simple matter before the Court of Law. He took time off to indicate that the specific order which he has given for the disclosure of documents would be acceptable to any Judge. He also went out of his way to indicate that the Statutory Instrument presented to the House of Assembly was extremely VAGUE!

"In a moment of revelatory insight he upbraided the Crown Counsel Ms Veronica Cenac for not acknowledging that there was some sort of guarantee and made the devastating point that if the guarantee was not in effect then there would be absolutely no obligation to honour the debt. Immediately, the whole structure of the proceedings fell into place.

"In essence, what Justice Shanks was implying is that the disclosure of documents is the open sesame to this case. If there is a guarantee given to RBTT Bank for the disbursement of funds AND this guarantee has the approval of the House of Assembly, then Counsel must disclose the document and put an immediate bridle (or baboochete) in the mouth of the Claimant Barrister **Martinus François** for ever after!

"If, on the other hand, such cannot be produced there is a grave infringement and violation of the laws of the country. The tragedy of Rochamel could not be put in starker terms!

"It is this frightening scenario which would unleash the Armageddon aspects of the predicament. First of all the principal Law Maker in the land would be the Principal Law Breaker if the document is not produced. Immediately, the scene is set for removing an offending Minister or Ministers.

"In Barbados a few months ago, an apparently serious charge was made against Prime Minister Owen Arthur – a charge not unlike the Rochamel Affair. Prime Minister Arthur promptly called his accusers' bluff by saying: 'If you can produce the documents to prove this charge I will immediately resign in disgrace.'

"Such courage! Such boldness! Perhaps it was courage nurtured by innocence. St. Lucians yearned for a similar declaration on Rochamel. But alas!

"In the wake of a projected collapse of a guilty Regime in St. Lucia it would be almost impossible to substitute an alternative Government. Too many loopholes must be blocked and a massive package of reassurance must be put in place to restore the trust which the Armageddon would have destroyed.

"There must be changes to the Constitution which seems to give unlimited power to Prime Ministers. There must be elaborate provisions to ensure accountability and transparency in the process of Government. There will be a public outcry for the conviction and imprisonment of any Leader who appears to have perpetrated an outlandish and massive raid on the public purse.

"Punitive measures will be demanded to avoid a reoccurrence of this heinous crime against the people. The sheer heartlessness and insensitivity of tampering with a sum of money in the vicinity of EC$100 million of the people's money suggests a vicious disconnect between the leadership and the people.

"Voices will be raised demanding that Ministers of Government should be surcharged in the same way that civil servants are called to book. Political pundits will question whether massive mandates are instruments of temptation to venal Governments. They will naturally wonder whether intellectuals could be trusted to promote the cause of the ordinary man. They will further demand that the leaders serve a period of apprenticeship to demonstrate the colour of their thinking and the depth of their sincerity.

"In the tradition of the criminal law voters will try to establish whether there was the criterion of *mens rea* or purposeful criminal intention in the dark recesses of the Rochamel mind. Most of all, this Armageddon will unleash a demand for strong moral and ethical leadership in any succeeding Government.

"As the Court case goes through its paces and the utter hopelessness of our political structure confronts us, I am tempted to fall into reverie. Was this the dreaded catalyst which our country needed to shunt us away from tired structures and opportunistic ladder climbers? Is Armageddon our key to RECONSTRUCTION... UNITY and LOVE?"

July 26, 2003

And so it was a hard life for this man of destiny, St. Lucia's Marcus Brutus, formerly of the St. Lucia Forum, then the St. Lucia Labour Action Movement (SLAM), then the St. Lucia Labour Party, then the Progressive Labour Party, then the National Front and then, the Alliance. Such credentials would almost look impressive had it not been for the fact that he destroyed all of the above on the altar of his political ambition.

Some, not too charitable, critics so utterly lost patience with what they perceived as Brutus' overweening ambition as to condemn him outright. The firm conclusion to which this writer has come to is this: We ought not to sneer at single-minded determination to achieve high political office; that any man who is informed by a vision of a better society ought o fight with every legitimate weapon at his disposal to bring that society about.

The following article represents Brutus' final public statement, prior to entering Tapion hospital for his last days and ultimate death on September 28, 2003, after he had been diagnosed with pancreatic cancer. The impromptu interview was conducted on September 2, 2003 by Radio St. Lucia's Michael Gaspard.

"When you are confronted with mortality, you get a rather clearer vision of things. You notice all the time you have spent in politics and realize that political division has not done the people of the country much good. We have to try a new way; a way to bind the people and make them born again. This has to be done by credible people who are not only looking for votes; working alongside people from different religions.

"However, it must be people who cannot be accused of material self-interest. So now those who serve the country have to have a higher motive than just bread on the table – or looking for bread under the table! We have to do all the things in the society to make us spiritual and caring – one with another. We have to have an all-embracing Christian ideal to bring everybody together in the circumstances they work in. Then the country will virtually determine what the leadership will do for it.

"When you have a narrow leadership that is only concerned with staying in power for the next election or canvassing a vote here and there; sometimes that generates negative reactions with the community. The people have to have the confidence that politicians in power are not conning them, while putting money in their pockets. In St. Lucia, politicians need a new credibility. They need to utilize the important spiritual leaders in our society.

"If God gave me strength to continue any kind of work, I would be in a completely new dimension. I would not be knocking down things; but bringing people together around a solid core of Christian values, based on peace, love and togetherness – with the emphasis on family and community.

"We need to forget the divisive politics. And for many years that's what I have been trying to do. A lot of people misunderstood me. They thought that I was looking for the Prime-Ministership and all kinds of nonsense like that. I was not after any Prime Minister position.

"What I have done in my political life have looked crazy many times. It's not. It is always inspired – and not for my own interests. In the work I did I was always cognizant that Christ was the greatest revolutionary on the face of the earth. So in all our fights in the Valleys we never encouraged violence or had anything like that. We were always trying to bind the people together.

"In my life, I have put my people and my country above my family and above friends who were close to me. My vision and mission involved the broad mass of people in St. Lucia whom we have to push forward for the betterment of this society.

"Fidel Castro is the greatest statesman on the face of the earth (even as Mandela is the greatest inspiration); and he is one of the most humane men I have ever met. Castro, under very challenging conditions, is taking care of the basic infrastructure of his country as best he could – especially in free access to health and education for all. Imagine that you don't have to fight to send your children to school and to get schoolbooks – or even to send your children to university.

"It is true in Cuba that there is struggle and hardship; but the people can survive. For even if they are not working they are able to eat! We need to tackle St. Lucia's development along those lines – not in making deals with hoteliers and that kind of thing! The line of development should be about making our people strong.

"The people of this country should feel that those working for them are working strongly in their interest. They should not feel that they have a Government with personal axes to grind. As a Government, you don't even need to have a lot of good works to show the people if they can sense your credibility.

"If, when I spoke in the Budget speeches, the Government had heeded what I was saying about the rumblings on the ground and about the people of St. Lucia, the Government could survive with half of the projects which they have there now. The people have to have the feeling that you are genuinely taking care of them and their interests and that you are not getting greedy and more acquisitive. Also, the media should not be used just to push the interests of the Government, but to explore the creative possibilities of this community.

"To move forward, Government must form an alliance with all the main spiritual leaders in the country – Baptist, Adventist, Pentecostal, Charismatic, Roman Catholic, Anglican, Methodist, and Non-denominational.

"Take all of them and bring them together and let them pull this community together, hand-in-hand with the political directorship. For if the political directorship is confident enough to allow the spiritual leaders to mobilize the people, it can be done. I was trying that politically with the Alliance. But awah!

"That's where the spirituality comes in – and that's the way to go now.

"And so, I will talk to you another day when I feel stronger...."

The Crusader Newspaper: December 24, 2003

As Shakespeare's *Julius Caesar* closes, it highlights the close connection between "tragic mistake and a perception of things that are not". After all, the silver-haired sage Cicero warned the audience from the beginning: "Indeed, it is a strange disposed time/But men may construe things after their fashion/Clean from the purpose of the things themselves."

And Titinus might well have been referring to our Brutus when he says to the dead Cassius lying on the ground: "Alas, thou has misconstrued everything." As for Shakespeare's Brutus himself, "defeated and brought to bay with his poor remains of friends", he senses this is no accident of fate but the working out of the destiny to which he had long before committed himself: "Night hangs upon mine eyes, my bones would rest/That have but laboured to attain this hour."

Because of his "crime" against the establishment, success will now go to the calculating and opportunistic ANTHONY who inherits Brutus' followers and makes the final disposition; no matter he initiates no action but simply waits to gather the fallen fruit. In such a universe, one's chances of success are in direct proportion to one's skill in seizing his chances.

Our Brutus might best be compared to a gun-happy outlaw – free with the trigger but not very accurate in his aim. It is true that he began more than he was able to finish; but few would doubt that he has at least succeeded in sowing the seeds of social justice and social change in the body politic. However, socialism need not cease to offer change but it should, nevertheless, cease to frighten those who may not be its natural allies:

BRUTUS: *Romans, countrymen, and lovers!*
Hear me for my cause, and be silent, that you
may hear.
Believe me for mine honour, and have respect to
mine honour, that you may believe.

Censure me in your wisdom, and awake your senses, that you may the better judge.

If there be any in this assembly, any dear friend of Caesar's, to him I say that Brutus' love to Caesar was no less than his.

If then that friend demand why Brutus rose against Caesar, this is my answer;

Not that I lov'd Caesar less, but that I lov'd Rome more.

Had you rather Caesar were living, and die all slaves, than that Caesar were dead, to live all free men?

As Caesar lov'd me, I weep for him; as he was fortunate, I rejoiced at it, as he was valiant, I honour him; as he was ambitious, I slew him. There is tears for his love; joy for his fortune: honour for his valour; and death for his ambition.

Shakespeare's *Julius Caesar*: Act III, Scene II

St. Lucia's Marcus Brutus has, at the very least, provided the inspiration and the intellectual starting point for the Joshua generation of St. Lucians who may yet lead St. Lucia out of neo-colonial bondage and into the Promised Land.

EPILOGUE II
ST. LUCIA'S JULIUS CAESAR

... After all, who will deny [Julius Caesar] – never mind the self-serving critical life reviews, my own, chief among them – yes, who will say that the hand of [Caesar], in one way or another, has not touched every single living soul in St. Lucia. Yes, touched us in ways that Derek Walcott never could; never will. Ditto Sir Arthur Lewis. George Charles? [Brutus]? Finally, both amount to no more than players, albeit in lead roles, in [Caesar's] legend. Julian Hunte too. As for any other name to ancient to immediately recall, whatever their sterling contributions, it was [Caesar] who, for better or for worse, had carried the baton to the finish line. What passes for education in our country – yes, yes, expect me to be typically hard; I'm also consistent – has to be credited to [St. Lucia's Julius Caesar]. We have no other choice. And lest we point only to the multitudinous illiterates and subliterates, let us also admit that our lawyers, doctors, architects, and so on, their offspring too, all got their education in [Caesar's] time as leader of this nation. Bananas (and no, I have not forgotten Julius and Randy Joseph!) and our economy, never mind the political blatherskites, have never fared better than in [Caesar's] time. Our infrastructure, social and otherwise, the basic

installation and facilities on which our growth depends, yes, chalk all of this up to [Caesar].

Rick Wayne: Star Newspaper Article entitled "St. Lucia's Man of the Century" (December 31, 1999)

The 1979 SLP Government disintegrated in late 1981 and by the middle of 1982, Caesar's "ghost" was back again running St. Lucia. But the return of Caesar's ghost was anything but a vote of confidence in Caesar. In fact, St. Lucians were more disenchanted with Brutus and his followers than enchanted with Caesar:

ANTHONY: Caesar's spirit, raging for revenge,
With Ate by his side, come hot from hell,
Shall in these confines, with a Monarch's voice
Cry "Havoc!" and let slip the dogs of war.

Shakespeare's *Julius Caesar*: Act III, Scene I

He won the elections in 1987 and 1992 respectively but was forced to give up power in 1996 to his chosen successor, Dr. Vaughan Lewis, the then director of the Organization of Eastern Caribbean States (OECS)), after he had ordered his Special Services Unit (SSU) of the police force, his perennial agents of tyranny, to open fire on a crowd of peacefully demonstrating banana farmers in the Valleys, killing Randy Joseph and Julius Joseph and seriously wounding and injuring scores of others as they were running for their lives; conveniently forgetting his 1950s histrionics in the same Valleys:

BRUTUS: But 'tis common proof
That lowliness is young ambition's ladder;
Whereto the climber-upward turns his face;
But when he once attains the upmost rung,
He then unto the ladder turns his back,

> *Looks in the clouds, scorning the base degrees*
> *By which he did ascend.*

Shakespeare's *Julius Caesar*: Act II, Scene I

But to have claimed in 1996, when he handed over power to Vaughan Lewis, that for him all passion was now spent would have been to claim too much. Aware of the writing on the wall in 1996 for his gross failure to treat with St. Lucia's social and economic problems, he was simply doing everything within his power to postpone the final Armageddon for his party. And he had no intention of quitting yet – he loved himself too much and loved power even more.

The following article, dated May 24, 2003, written by Caesar, was circulated to the local media thus:

"THE P.M. MUST GO, SAYS SIR JOHN

"I promised not to make statements except on issues of national importance and to defend my record in office. The Rochamel/Hyatt issue is considered to be one such issue which demands my intervention.

"The Prime Minister's statement on this matter is both inadequate and in some important respects inaccurate and it confirms the saying 'Oh what a tangled web we weave, when first we practice to deceive.'

"In seeking to extricate himself of the tangled web of deception, the Prime Minister engaged us for two hours on I.P.I., repeated one night later on H.T.S.

"The Prime Minister in his attempt to confuse sought to compare the Rochamel/Hayatt issue with that of the Jalousie/Hilton. There can be no comparison. In the Jalousie/Hilton case, for the US$5 million invested in the hotel, Government received 25% of the shares in that hotel which at that time was valued in excess of US$52 million.

"The Government did not burden the taxpayers with any debt whatsoever but received assets valued in excess of US$12 million.

"I would like to state the circumstances which led to Government's intervention. In 1995, the Jalousie/Hilton ran into serious financial problems and after the owners refused to pump any more money into the venture, the hotel was closed, putting over 200 persons, employees, and those who were dependant on it, out of work and leaving a trail of debts both local and external.

"In order to save the jobs and to get this hotel operational, the Government and the owners went in search of a buyer. One hotel operator which showed interest was the Hilton chain. For the first time, there would be an internationally recognized name operating a hotel in St. Lucia. They are merely operators, not owners.

"In this case, however, they were persuaded to invest US$5 million to upgrade the Jalousie hotel and accept an equity position. Another problem was the debt of the hotel. These must be paid. They included severance pay and holiday pay to the workers, N.I.S. payments, Hotel Occupancy Tax and PAYE owed to the Government and payment owed to local suppliers of goods and services.

"In return for shares in the hotel, Government agreed to assume the debts owed to local suppliers and to pay severance and holiday pay to the workers. The suppliers who were owed up to EC$10,000 were paid in full and those in excess of EC$10,000 were paid 70% of the debt. No foreign debt was accepted and paid for by the Government. These agreements were agreed to in consultation with the Chamber of Commerce, the Unions and the N.I.S.

"There was a shortfall of US$1 million on Government's contribution and this was made up by the transfer of US$ 1 million from an account held in the Mabouya Valley account for the sale of Crown Lands in the Mabouya Valley. Quite a lot has been said about this, but it was money owed to the Government from the sale of lands on the Dennery Estates acquired by Government.

"This hotel was refurbished and opened in 1998, in time for the CARICOM Heads of Government Conference in July of that year and was the showpiece to host such dignitaries as President Mandela of South Africa and other Heads of State and Government.

"For an investment of US$5 million Government has 25% shares in a property now valued in excess of US$75 million, with two members on the Board of Directors and over 300 persons directly or indirectly benefiting from the hotel.

"Let us compare this with the Rochamel/Hyatt Hotel deal and the web of deception which has followed.

"In 1997 the S.L.P Government headed by Dr. Kenny Anthony continued with the Hyatt negotiation for management of a hotel on the Pigeon Island Causeway. These negotiations had commenced under the U.W.P. Government. As part of the deal agreed to by Kenny Anthony's Government, was the meeting of the cost overruns on the construction of the hotel, even before the construction had started.

"This gave the Rochamel Company, the company involved in the construction, a blank cheque drawn on the treasury of St. Lucia. This deal was kept secret until the bomb burst in the year 2000 after the hotel went into bankruptcy and was put up for sale.

"The price paid by Sandals is not known, but Sandals was informed that there was an outstanding amount of US$15 million on the hotel as a result of cost overruns guaranteed by the Government of St. Lucia, and demanded that this debt be settled before the sale was completed.

"The Bank, R.B.T.T., then called on the Government to meet its obligations. This agreement which was never brought before the Parliament of St. Lucia is a gross violation of the Finance and Audit Act, and therefore is not worth the paper on which it is written. It is completely useless.

"In an attempt to validate it, the Prime Minister was forced to seek the approval of Parliament five years after the event. But even then he sought to continue his deception by hiding it in a Resolution for 'Capital Works and Incidental Matters'. Is $30 million worth of debts to be paid by the people of St. Lucia an 'incidental matter'?

"And this, from a Government which boasted 'transparency and accountability'?

"Not only is this secret agreement a gross violation of the laws of St. Lucia, but no attempt was made by the Kenny Anthony Government to protect the interest of the people of St. Lucia by having on site a professional person verifying any claim of 'cost overrun'.

"Who, on behalf of Government, has audited the Rochamel books to ensure that the monies said to have been spent on the project were actually spent? The Prime Minister has not told us. Where is the vaunted accountability?

"Now the people of this country must pay in excess of $42 million or $1 million every month for which they have received nothing in return. This cannot be accepted.

"Many of those people and organizations who were in the past rather vocal are now completely silent. We should recall the demand by the Chamber of Commerce, the Christian Council and other organizations for the appointment of a Commission of Inquiry into what they termed the 'U.N. Funds Scandal'.

"Where are their voices now in the face of his outrage? So gross is the violation of the laws of this country, that Dr. Anthony, as a Minister of Finance, can no longer be trusted with the finances of this country, therefore HE MUST GO and with him his band of looters who have reduced this once proud and prosperous country to this pitiful state in which it now finds itself.

"The web of deceit must end. This Government MUST GO. According to one of them in the 1997 Elections, ENOUGH IS ENOUGH.

"One should contrast this with the treatment given to William Charles of AMERICAN DRYWALL who appealed for assistance of US$4 million in return for 25% ownership in his Crowne Plaza Hotel project in which he had already invested substantial sums of money. This was refused and the entire DRYWALL venture was pushed into liquidation, but the US$15 million to Rochamel can be paid and we get nothing in return, except the burden.

"Yet the Government continues to weave the strands of deception and in order to distract public attention, the Prime Minister states that the U.W.P. Government made no provision for the public in the Pigeon Island Causeway Project. This is false and the Prime Minister knows it to be false.

"Four acres on the Pigeon Island end were reserved for the public and a further three acres on the Gros Islet side. These reservations are recorded in the St. Lucia Gazette, and are available in the Ministry of Planning. Surely, the Prime Minister should be aware of this.

"The Prime Minister was emphatic that he will defend himself and his record. This is his right. He should also respect the rights and records of those who served before him and verify his statements before subjecting the Nation to his diatribe."

For his "band of looters" statement quoted above, Caesar was successfully sued by ANTHONY for libel. He grabbed power again in 2006 but lasted less than a year – he died with power in his hands on September 7, 2007.

The question of Caesar's succession has been a cause of much interregnum in the UWP, which Caesar dominated since its inception in 1964 to such an extent that to imagine the UWP without Caesar is to imagine Shakespeare's *Julius Caesar* without the Roman Julius Caesar.

Political leaders, especially in the post-colonial Caribbean, are always wary of grooming new cadres of leadership for eventual succession. They are not in the Civil Service with compulsory retirement at 65. Nor was St. Lucia's Julius Caesar the first Prime Minister to work on the assumption that he could go on in power forever; or, at least, such a prospect would not be assisted by naming an heir apparent. So in order to satisfy his own insecurities, he always surrounded himself with minions as Ministers; cocooned in the knowledge that such persons did not possess the intellectual legitimacy to issue a challenge to his hegemony – never mind they never brought any positive strengths to his administrations:

CAESAR: *Let me have men about me that are fat;*
Sleek-headed men and such as sleep o'nights;
Young Cassius has a lean and hungry look;
He thinks too much; such men are dangerous.

Shakespeare's *Julius Caesar*: Act I, Scene II

Ironically, the UWP's greatest strength since 1964, Caesar, has been its greatest weakness. Indeed, the most obvious weakness of UWP rule has been its failure to breed a species of politician capable of taking advantage of this moment in its history. For the United Workers' Party, Caesar's long-term autocracy will leave a terrible legacy; it faces a perilously insecure future – a famine may follow the feast.

> THE LIGHT OF
>
> THE NEW ST. LUCIA MODEL
>
> WILL ILLUMINE THIS LAND
>
> AND A NEW BREED OF MAN
>
> WILL EMERGE
>
> TO GRAPPLE
>
> WITH THE PROBLEM OF FORGING
>
> A NEW AND JUST SOCIETY